I0789476

The Zine Maker's Handbook

A Complete Guide to Creating, Publishing, and Distributing Your DIY Zine from Cut-and-Paste to Digital PDFs

Casey Miller

AKASHA PRESS

THE ZINE MAKER'S HANDBOOK
CASEY MILLER
AKASHA PRESS
13/02/2026

The Zine Maker's Handbook

That First Zine Feeling: Welcome to the World of DIY Publishing

I was seventeen and adrift in a sea of suburban boredom when I found it. Tucked away in the corner of a dusty independent record store, on a wire rack usually reserved for free local papers, was a stack of flimsy, photocopied booklets. They were crookedly stapled and unapologetically messy. One had a hand-drawn, angry-looking cat on the cover with the words "CAPITALISM IS A CAT-ASTROPHE" scrawled above it in Sharpie. Another was just a collage of old family photos with typed-out poetry. I picked one up. It was thin, maybe eight pages folded from a single sheet of paper, and it felt impossibly fragile and powerful at the same time.

The paper was still warm, or maybe I imagined it was, fresh from the copy machine at a Kinko's or a public library. The ink smelled slightly burnt. Inside was a rambling, passionate, and hilarious comic about the creator's terrible summer job at a fast-food restaurant. The drawings were crude, the lettering was uneven, but the voice was so clear, so authentic, it felt like I was reading a secret letter from a friend I hadn't met yet. I bought it for a dollar, a transaction that felt more like an act of solidarity than a purchase. Holding that zine, I felt a spark. It wasn't just a booklet; it was a message in a bottle, a signal flare sent up from someone else's island of weirdness, and it told me I wasn't alone.

That's the magic of it. That's the first zine feeling. It's the jolt of recognition when you hold a handmade object that contains a piece of someone's soul. This book is about bottling that feeling—first as a reader, and then, most importantly, as a creator.

What Happens When You Hold a Zine for the First Time

If you've never held a zine, the experience can be a little disorienting at first. We're accustomed to media that is polished, perfect, and produced by invisible corporations. A magazine has glossy, airbrushed photos and articles written by a team of editors. A book has a stiff spine, a professional cover design, and an ISBN number. A website has been focus-grouped and A/B tested to optimize user engagement. A zine has none of that. And that's its superpower.

When you pick up a zine, the first thing you notice is its physicality. You feel the specific weight and tooth of the paper the creator chose—or, more likely, what was available and cheap. You see the ghost-like imperfections of the photocopy, the slight misalignment of the pages, the industrial clench of the staples. You might even see a fingerprint smudge in the toner. These aren't flaws. They are proof of life. They are the marks of a human hand and a singular vision, untouched by a marketing department or a board of directors.

Then there's the content itself. A zine can be about anything. Literally anything. I've read zines that were detailed guides to the best public bathrooms in Portland, Oregon. I've read a zine that was a heartbreakingly beautiful photo essay about a dying houseplant. I've read zines filled with angry political manifestos, collections of vegan recipes, fan fiction about obscure 80s television shows, and deeply personal comics about mental health. There are no rules. The only barrier to entry is the cost of a few photocopies.

This lack of rules is what makes the experience so intimate. Reading a zine feels like being let in on a secret. The voice is unfiltered, direct, and personal. It's not trying to sell you anything or appeal to the widest possible demographic. It's one person saying, "This is what I care about. This is what I'm obsessed with. This is what keeps me up at night." In a world saturated with disingenuous content created by algorithms for clicks, the raw honesty of a zine is a radical act. It's a quiet but firm rejection of the idea that our stories, our passions, and our perspectives are only valuable if they can be monetized or go viral.

Holding a zine for the first time is to be reminded that media can be human-scale. It's a connection forged not through a screen, but through paper and ink and staples. It's a tangible piece of a subculture, a community, a friendship. You are holding a conversation you've been invited to join.

More Than Just a Booklet: Why Zines are a Powerful Form of Expression

It's easy to dismiss zines as a quaint hobby, a relic from a pre-internet era. Just flimsy paper pamphlets in a world of digital everything. But to do so is to miss the point entirely. Zines have always been, and continue to be, one of the most vital and accessible forms of independent publishing. They are tools of communication, community-building, and sometimes, revolution.

Their power comes from their freedom from gatekeepers. Think about what it takes to get a book published, an article placed in a major magazine, or a film produced. It requires agents, editors, publishers, and investors. It requires convincing a series of people that your idea is commercially viable. It's a system designed to be exclusive, to filter out voices that are too strange, too niche, too unprofitable, or too dangerous. Zines blow a hole right through that system. A zine doesn't need anyone's approval. All it needs is a creator with something to say and a way to make copies.

This is why zines have been so crucial to so many social and cultural movements. In the 1930s and 40s, science fiction fans created the first zines to discuss stories and build communities outside the confines of mainstream magazines. In the 1970s, punk zines like Sniffin' Glue in the UK captured the raw energy and DIY ethos of the music scene in a way no established music press ever could. They didn't just report on the culture; they were the culture, created by the same kids who were in the bands and in the audience.

Perhaps most famously, in the 1990s, zines were the lifeblood of the Riot Grrrl movement. Young women, fed up with the sexism of the punk scene and society at large, picked up scissors, glue sticks, and pens. They created zines like Bikini Kill and Jigsaw to talk about feminism, body image, sexuality, and survival. These zines weren't just about sharing ideas; they were about creating networks of support and solidarity. A girl in a small town in Ohio could send a dollar and a stamp and receive a zine from Olympia, Washington, that told her she wasn't crazy, she wasn't alone, and that her anger was valid. In an era before social media, this was a lifeline. It was a way for a marginalized community to speak for itself, to itself.

That legacy continues today. In our hyper-digital age, the physical, tangible nature of a zine is more potent than ever. A social media post is ephemeral, lost in the endless scroll. A zine is an object. It can be held, saved, passed along. Zine fests, where creators gather to sell and trade their work, are vibrant hubs of real-world community that a comments section can never replicate. In a world of carefully curated online personas, the messy, imperfect honesty of a zine feels more authentic and necessary than ever. It's a small, quiet, paper-based rebellion against the noise.

This Book is Your Permission Slip to Create (No Experience Necessary)

At this point, a little voice might be whispering in your ear. It's a familiar voice, the one that pops up whenever you get a creative impulse. It's the voice of self-doubt. It's probably saying things like: "This is all very interesting, but I could never do that. I'm not an artist. I'm not a writer. I don't have anything important to say. My life isn't interesting enough."

I would like you to find that little voice, thank it for its concern, and then politely tell it to shut up. Because it is wrong. Completely, totally, one-hundred-percent wrong. The belief that you need to be a special kind of person—an "Artist" with a capital A—to create something is the biggest lie the gatekeepers ever sold us. It's a lie designed to keep you a passive consumer instead of an active creator.

This book is your official, notarized, gold-embossed permission slip. Permission to be messy. Permission to be imperfect. Permission to make something that isn't for everyone. Permission to create something just for the sheer, unadulterated joy of it. You do not need a fine arts degree. You do not need to know how to draw a straight line. You do not need to have lived a wildly adventurous life. You just need a point of view.

My first zine was a disasterpiece. I made it when I was seventeen, right after that fateful trip to the record store. It was about my love for old monster movies. I typed the text on my mom's ancient typewriter, complete with typos I corrected with Wite-Out. The pictures were fuzzy images I photocopied directly from a book I checked out of the library (please don't tell the librarian). I didn't know how to lay it out properly, so the pages were in the wrong order. I stapled it all together crookedly. It was, by any objective measure, a mess. And I have never been prouder of anything in my entire life.

Making that zine was liberating because the goal wasn't to create a masterpiece. The goal was simply to make it. It was to take the love and enthusiasm I had for something and give it a physical form. The zine community isn't about technical perfection; it's about passion. Do you love baking bread? Are you obsessed with a particular bird that visits your backyard? Do you have strong feelings about the designated hitter rule in baseball? Do you want to share your grandmother's stories? That's your zine. Your passion, your unique perspective, is the only qualification you need.

So let go of the idea that you have nothing to say. You have a lifetime of experiences, thoughts, and opinions that are uniquely yours. Zine making is simply a process of excavating those things and sharing them. It's not about being an expert; it's about being an enthusiast. And everyone is an enthusiast about something.

What to Expect: A Messy, Fun, and Rewarding Journey into Zine Making

So, you have your permission slip. What happens now? What does this creative road trip actually look like? Well, I can promise you it won't be a neat and tidy affair. It will be messy. There will almost certainly be glue on your fingers and paper scraps all over your floor. There will be moments of frustration and moments of unexpected discovery.

Making your first zine is a bit like learning to cook a new dish without a perfect, step-by-step recipe. This book will be your kitchen guide. We'll stock the pantry together, showing you the basic ingredients: paper, pens, scissors, glue, a photocopier. We'll talk about different cooking methods—the quick and simple one-page zine, the more complex stitched-spine booklet, the digital PDF zine. But you are the chef. You get to decide what you're making.

The process will start in your head and in your notebooks. We'll spend time figuring out what you're passionate about, what story is itching to be told. This is the brainstorming phase, where no idea is too silly or too small. It's about gathering your raw materials—your words, your drawings, your photos, your collages. It's a treasure hunt through your own mind.

Then comes the hands-on part, the wonderful, tactile magic of putting it all together. You'll learn the simple alchemy of folding a single sheet of paper in just the right way to create a tiny, eight-page book. You'll feel the satisfying snip of scissors cutting through paper and the sticky pull of a glue stick. You might wrestle with a finicky printer or a copy machine that keeps jamming. This is all part of it. These aren't obstacles; they're part of the story of your zine's creation. Each struggle adds to its handmade charm.

Finally, there's the moment of truth: holding your finished zine. You'll have a stack of them, maybe ten, maybe fifty, all smelling of fresh toner. You'll have created a multiple of an original object. You'll have made something that can be shared, traded, and sent out into the world. And that's where the final part of the adventure begins—connecting with others. Putting your zine into someone else's hands is a thrill unlike any other. It's the culmination of your journey, the moment your personal act of creation becomes a public act of communication.

This is a path of play and experimentation. It is not a straight line, but a meandering walk through a forest of ideas. Along the way, you won't just learn how to make a booklet. You'll learn how to pay closer attention to the world around you, how to articulate your own voice, and how to find the courage to share it. It's a messy, fun, and profoundly rewarding process. So roll up your sleeves. It's time to make a beautiful mess.

That first zine feeling—the spark you get from holding someone else's passion project—is a powerful thing. But it's nothing compared to the feeling of seeing someone else's eyes light up when they read the zine you made. That's the real magic. It's the moment you stop being just a reader and become part of the conversation. Welcome to the club. Let's get started.

From Sci-Fi Fans to Riot Grrrls: The Rebel History of Zines

That messy, photocopied booklet I found in the record store felt like a secret just for me. It was a tiny island of weirdness in a sea of suburban sameness. But as I peeled back the crookedly stapled pages, I wasn't just discovering one person's strange and wonderful brain; I was unknowingly tapping into a long, vibrant, and fiercely independent history. That zine wasn't a random fluke. It was the latest dispatch from a secret war against silence, a tradition of self-publishing passed down through generations of outsiders, dreamers, and rebels.

It's a history that doesn't get taught in schools, and you won't find it in most official accounts of media or literature. This is a story written on cheap paper with borrowed ink, passed hand-to-hand in basements, at shows, and in the dusty corners of record stores just like the one I wandered into. It's the story of how everyday people, armed with nothing more than an idea and a way to make copies, built entire worlds, forged communities, and screamed their truths when no one else would give them a microphone. To understand the power of that little booklet, you have to understand the renegades who paved the way.

The Proto-Zines: Pamphleteers, Poets, and Early Amateurs

Long before anyone had heard the word "zine," the spirit was already there. Think about it: at its core, a zine is a self-published work created outside of mainstream channels, designed to spread a particular idea, passion, or perspective to a niche audience. If we use that definition, the family tree of zines grows deep and wild, stretching back centuries. Its earliest ancestors were the firebrands and agitators, the people who couldn't—or wouldn't—wait for an official printing press to approve their message.

In 1776, Thomas Paine's pamphlet Common Sense functioned as the era's equivalent of a blog or a Twitter thread. It was crudely printed and sold for pennies, but it was written in the language of the people. The pamphlet bypassed the British-controlled press and spoke directly to farmers, merchants, and artisans, arguing for something unthinkable: independence. Paine was, in a way, the ultimate political zinester. He had a radical message, an urgent need to share it, and he used the most accessible technology of his day to get it into people's hands. His work was not about profit; it was about sparking a revolution.

This same spirit pulsed through other movements. The Dadaists in the early 20th century, disgusted by the logic that led to World War I, spewed out manifestos and bizarre, collage-filled journals that defied all artistic conventions. The Beat poets in the 1950s, like Allen Ginsberg, initially self-published works like Howl in small, chapbook formats because no mainstream publisher would touch their raw, honest, and controversial content. Each of these acts was a refusal to be silenced. They were all saying, in their own way, "If you won't publish us, we'll do it ourselves." They were laying the groundwork, proving that you don't need permission to have a voice.

The Mothers and Fathers of It All: Science Fiction Fandom in the 1930s

While the spirit is ancient, the zine as we know it has a clear and wonderfully nerdy birthplace: the world of science fiction fandom. In the 1930s, pulp magazines like Amazing Stories were portals to other galaxies for thousands of readers. These weren't just passive consumers; they were passionate, intelligent fans who wanted to do more than just read the stories. They wanted to discuss them, critique them, and even write their own. They started writing letters to the magazines, which would be published in columns in the back. Soon, fans were writing letters to each other, their addresses pulled from the very pages of the pulps.

It didn't take long for someone to have a brilliant idea. Instead of just writing one-on-one letters, why not collect all these letters, reviews, and fan-written stories into a single publication and send it out to everyone? In 1930, the Science Correspondence Club produced a publication called The Comet. It was a collection of typed pages, created by fans, for fans. They called it a "fan magazine," and the term was quickly shortened to "fanzine." And right there, the zine was born.

These early fanzines were labors of love. Picture a young man in Cleveland in 1935, hunched over a clunky typewriter in his parents' attic, painstakingly typing out stencils. He's writing an essay arguing why H.G. Wells is superior to Jules Verne, illustrating it with a shaky ink drawing of a rocket ship. He's not doing it for money or fame. He's doing it to connect with a dozen other people scattered across the country who get it. These fanzines were their social network. They were filled with passionate arguments, inside jokes, and a shared vocabulary. They created a community where there was none before, linking isolated enthusiasts into a vibrant, intellectual subculture. This is where the core DNA of zine culture was formed: community, passion, and a do-it-yourself ethos.

The Mimeo Revolution: When Copying Became an Art Form

For these early sci-fi fans, the biggest hurdle was technology. How do you make copies without a professional printing press? The answer came in the form of a clunky, ink-stained machine that would become a patron saint of self-publishers for decades: the mimeograph. If you've ever smelled a freshly printed worksheet from an old school and gotten a whiff of that distinct, slightly sweet chemical smell, you've experienced the mimeo's legacy.

Using a mimeograph was a messy, physical process. You'd type or draw onto a special wax paper stencil, which would create a template. Then you'd attach this stencil to a rotating drum on the machine, load it with ink, and hand-crank the handle. With each turn, a roller would press paper against the inked stencil, squeezing ink through the tiny perforations to create a copy. The result was often a bit blurry, the ink a distinctive purple or blue, and your hands would be stained for days. But it worked. For the first time, you could produce a hundred copies of something for a tiny fraction of the cost of professional printing.

This "Mimeo Revolution," as it came to be known, was a massive democratizing force. Suddenly, anyone with access to one of these machines—often found in offices, schools, or churches—could become a publisher. The technology spread beyond science fiction, fueling the underground press of the 1960s. Activists used mimeo machines to print anti-war leaflets and civil rights newsletters. Poets cranked out collections of their work to sell at readings. The machine itself became a symbol of grassroots communication. It was slow, imperfect, and messy, but it gave a voice to those who had been voiceless. It was the humble, mechanical engine that powered counterculture.

Punk Rock & The Photocopier: How the 70s and 80s Exploded Zine Culture

If the mimeograph was the quiet, steady engine of the first wave, the photocopier was pure rocket fuel. When affordable, high-speed copy machines—particularly the Xerox 914—started showing up in libraries, copy shops, and offices in the late 1970s, it changed everything. The slow, messy process of the mimeo was replaced by the instant, electric hum of the copier. And this technological leap coincided perfectly with a cultural explosion: punk rock.

The ethos of punk was fundamentally DIY. You didn't need to be a virtuoso to be in a band; you just needed three chords and something to say. That same spirit was immediately applied to publishing. The message was clear: you don't need to be a journalist to start a magazine. You just need a glue stick, a pair of scissors, a Sharpie, and access to a photocopier (preferably for free, after hours at your boring office job). The result was an unprecedented explosion of zines.

The aesthetic of punk zines was a direct reflection of the music and the technology. It was raw, immediate, and confrontational. Pages were chaotic collages of cut-out letters from newspapers, creating the iconic "ransom note" look. Photos were grainy, high-contrast images, often shot at shows and developed on the cheap. The writing was visceral and opinionated, full of misspelled words and passionate rants. Zines like Sniffin' Glue in the UK and Slash in Los Angeles weren't just reporting on the punk scene; they were the punk scene. They were the forums for arguing about which bands sold out, the place to find out about a secret show, and the way to read an interview with your favorite band that was as raw and unfiltered as their music.

This was the era that truly solidified the zine as a tool of subcultural identity. Every town with a punk scene had its own zines. They were the connective tissue, the primary way that music, fashion, and ideas spread in a pre-internet world. You'd buy them at shows, trade them through the mail, and use them to discover new bands and new friends. Making a zine was a political act—a rejection of slick, corporate magazines and a declaration that your voice, your scene, and your opinions mattered.

Riot Grrrl: The Personal Becomes Political (and Photocopied)

By the early 1990s, the punk scene, which had started as a haven for misfits, had become in many ways just another boys' club. The mosh pits were aggressive and male-dominated, and the lyrics often ignored or were hostile to women's experiences. In response to this, a new, fiercely feminist movement erupted from within the punk underground: Riot Grrrl. And their weapon of choice was the zine.

Riot Grrrls took the DIY ethos of punk and turned it inward, championing the idea that "the personal is political." Zines became intimate, confessional spaces where young women could write about topics that were completely absent from mainstream media and even from the male-dominated punk zines. They wrote about sexism in the scene, body image, eating disorders, sexual assault, friendship, and incandescent rage. The photocopier became a tool for consciousness-raising. A girl in Olympia, Washington, could write a searingly honest account of her daily life, make a hundred copies, and through mail-based distribution networks, connect with another girl in a small town in Pennsylvania who read it and thought, for the first time, I am not alone.

The aesthetics shifted, too. While the cut-and-paste style of punk remained, Riot Grrrl zines were often more personal. They featured handwritten diary entries, vulnerability mixed with fury, collages of childhood photos next to angry manifestos. Zines with names like Bikini Kill (created by the band of the same name), Jigsaw, and Girl Germs were more than just fan publications; they were lifelines. They built a nationwide, and eventually worldwide, community of solidarity. They encouraged girls to start their own bands, to create their own art, and to speak their own truths without apology.

This was the direct heritage of the angry-cat zine that I'd picked up. The scrawled Sharpie, the unapologetic politics, the feeling that it was a message in a bottle from one person's reality to mine—it all came from the revolutionary spirit of Riot Grrrl. They proved that a zine could be a diary, a manifesto, a work of art, and a call to arms, all at once.

Zines Today: The Enduring Power of Paper in a Digital World

So, what happened? The internet arrived. Blogs, LiveJournal, and eventually social media platforms offered a seemingly better way to do everything zines did. You could publish instantly, reach a global audience for free, and build communities through forums and comment sections. For a while, it seemed like the photocopied zine might finally go the way of the mimeograph and become a historical curiosity.

But a funny thing happened. Zines didn't die. In fact, in many ways, they are thriving. Why? Because in a world of endless scrolling, ephemeral content, and algorithmic feeds, the physical zine offers a powerful antidote. It's an act of deliberate creation and consumption. You can't accidentally stumble upon a zine; you have to seek it out at a zine fest, buy it from an artist, or get it in the mail. It's a finite object. It won't be updated, it won't serve you ads, and it won't disappear when a platform goes bankrupt.

Holding a zine today is a tactile rebellion. It's a connection to a real person who folded, stapled, and sent this thing out into the world. The variety is staggering. There are "perzines" (personal zines) that continue the Riot Grrrl tradition of intimate storytelling. There are art zines filled with beautiful illustrations and photography. There are zines about cooking, hiking, mental health, niche video games, and political activism. Zine fests have popped up in cities all over the world, acting as vibrant, temporary marketplaces for this incredible creative output.

The zine has survived because it offers something the internet can't: intimacy. It's a closed circuit between the creator and the reader. It's a quiet space in a loud world. It's a testament to the enduring human need to make something tangible, to hold our ideas in our hands, and to share them with someone else, hoping they understand.

From the revolutionary pamphleteer to the sci-fi nerd, from the snarling punk to the furious Riot Grrrl, the thread remains unbroken. It's a history of people deciding they have something important to say and finding a way to say it, no matter the odds. Every time someone sits down with a glue stick and a stack of paper, they are not just making a little booklet. They are joining a long, proud, and rebellious lineage of creators who dared to believe their voice mattered. They are keeping the secret history alive.

So, What's Your Zine About? Unearthing Your Passion

So, you're in. You've felt the pull of that photocopied magic. You've glimpsed the secret history of rebels and poets who refused to be silent. You're holding a blank sheet of paper, a pair of scissors, maybe a glue stick, and the revolutionary spirit is buzzing in your veins. And then, the loudest, most intimidating silence in the world descends. It's the silence of the blank page, and it asks a single, terrifying question: ...Now what?

This is the moment. It's the point where the romantic idea of being a zinester crashes into the stark reality of creation. It's the question I get asked more than any other, whispered in crowded zine fests and typed in late-night DMs: "I desperately want to make a zine, but I have no idea what to make it about." It's a question that carries the weight of a lifetime of being told our stories aren't important enough, our interests are too weird, and our passions aren't productive.

Let me tell you a secret that will dismantle that entire line of thinking: the question is not the barrier you think it is. It's the key. The fact that you're asking it means you're already halfway there. You have something to say; you just need to give yourself permission to say it. This chapter is that permission slip. We're going to dig through the treasure chest of your own mind and prove, once and for all, that you have an endless supply of material.

The Myth of the 'Good Idea' (Hint: They're All Good Ideas)

Before we even get into brainstorming, we need to perform an exorcism. We need to cast out the demon of the 'Good Idea.' This is the little voice in your head, the one that sounds suspiciously like a cynical high school teacher or a perpetually unimpressed boss, that insists your idea must be original, profound, commercially viable, and universally beloved before you even put pen to paper. In the world of zines, that voice is a liar.

My first real zine, after a few failed attempts at being profound, was about my intense, bordering-on-unhealthy relationship with the instant ramen section of my local Asian grocery store. That was it. I took blurry photos of the packaging. I wrote haikus about broth. I ranked the different spice packets. I drew a little cartoon of a noodle weeping with joy. On paper, it was a profoundly silly, pointless idea. It had no grand message about society. It wasn't going to win any awards. My 'Good Idea' demon was screaming at me that this was embarrassing.

But I made it anyway, because for some reason, I just had to. I printed twenty copies and left them at a local coffee shop. A week later, a barista I'd never spoken to pulled me aside and said, "Hey, you're the ramen zine person, right? I loved it. You totally get why the Shin Black is superior." In that moment, I didn't just feel seen; I felt like I had found a secret password to a club I didn't even know existed. The zine wasn't a masterpiece. But it was real. It was fueled by a genuine, albeit weird, passion. And that authenticity is the only currency that matters in this world.

A 'good idea' for a zine isn't an idea that will change the world. It's an idea that changes your world, even just for the afternoon it takes to make it. It's an idea that gets you excited enough to cut and paste and write and draw. A zine about the pigeons you see on your commute, a zine cataloging every dog you've ever petted, a zine of angry poems about your upstairs neighbor—these are all brilliant ideas. Why? Because they are yours. They are born from your life and your perspective. In zine-making, passion is the metric of quality. If you care about it, it's a good idea. End of story.

Brainstorming Exercise: The 'Brain Dump' Method for Endless Topics

Okay, so we've agreed to ignore the 'Good Idea' demon. Now what? We need to get our hands dirty. This isn't about waiting for a lightning bolt of inspiration to strike. Inspiration is a worker, not a muse, and she likes it when you meet her halfway. The best way to do that is with a technique so simple it feels like cheating: the brain dump.

Find a piece of paper, the bigger and messier the better. A notebook page works, but the back of a junk mail envelope or a sprawling piece of butcher paper is even better. This is not a time for your fancy leather-bound journal. This is a time for chaos. Now grab a pen and set a timer for ten minutes. For those ten minutes, your only job is to move your hand across the page. You are not allowed to stop, you are not allowed to judge, and you are not allowed to think too hard. You are simply creating a raw inventory of your own brain.

Start with simple lists. What do you love? Don't be poetic. Be specific. The smell of old books, the TV show Frasier, the way your cat's paws feel, that one specific bench in the park, synth-pop from 1983, the taste of cold pizza. Now, what do you hate? Again, be specific. The sound of people chewing, passive-aggressive emails, pants that are too tight, the concept of 'networking', weak coffee, movie trailers that spoil the whole plot.

Keep going. What are you obsessed with right now? A video game? A historical figure? A knitting pattern? A true-crime podcast? What questions are rattling around in your head? Why do we dream? Is it possible to be a good person under capitalism? Where do all the lost socks go? What's a memory you can't shake? The first time you rode a bike, a humiliating moment in middle school, a perfect summer day. What skills do you have? You can bake bread, you can identify five types of ferns, you can perfectly fold a fitted sheet, you can beat anyone at Mario Kart.

When the timer goes off, stop. Look at the glorious mess you've made. This isn't a to-do list; it's a map. It's a constellation of your personal universe. Somewhere in that chaotic scrawl of loves, hates, obsessions, and memories is not one zine idea, but a hundred. That list of things you love? Each one is a potential fanzine. That list of things you hate? That's a brilliant rant-zine waiting to happen. That skill you have? That's a how-to zine. That memory you can't shake? That is the heart of a powerful perzine.

Perzines: The Power of Your Own Story, Your Rants, Your Loves

The perzine is the soul of the zine world. Short for "personal zine," it is a zine about your own life, thoughts, and experiences. This is often the most intimidating category; many creators feel their lives are too boring to be of interest to others. In reality, these stories have a broad appeal, creating a powerful connection with readers who feel just as lost, just as boring, or just as weird.

A perzine is a declaration that your story matters. It's a rebellion against a culture that only seems to value the stories of the rich, the famous, and the conventionally successful. I once read a perzine that was just a hand-written account of the author's week working a soul-crushing retail job. It detailed the absurd customer complaints, the little moments of solidarity with co-workers, the exhaustion at the end of a shift. It was not dramatic. It was not glamorous. But it was so deeply, achingly human that I felt it in my bones. It made my own experiences in similar jobs feel validated and seen. The author hadn't written a story about a hero; she had written a story about a survivor, and in doing so, made all of us survivors feel a little less alone.

Your perzine can be anything. It can be a collection of diary entries, a rant about the state of modern dating, a love letter to your hometown, a chronicle of your journey with mental health, an essay about your relationship with your body, a comic about your daily anxieties. The power of the perzine lies in its specificity. Don't write about "love"; write about the time you held someone's hand for the first time and your palm was sweating. Don't write about "sadness"; write about the specific weight of a Tuesday afternoon when everything feels gray. The more personal and specific you are, the more universally resonant your story becomes.

Making a perzine is an act of radical vulnerability. It's scary. But it's also incredibly liberating. It's a way to process your own life, to find the narrative in your experiences, and to turn your internal monologue into a conversation. And when someone reads it and says, "Me too," you've created the most powerful connection art can make.

Fanzines: A Guide to Celebrating What You're Obsessed With

If perzines are about looking inward, fanzines are about looking outward with wide-eyed, unabashed joy. This is the genre that started it all, with those early science fiction fans geeking out about their favorite stories. Being a fan has been commercialized into oblivion—buy the t-shirt, the Funko Pop, the limited-edition collector's box. But the fanzine reclaims fandom as an active, creative pursuit. It's not about consumption; it's about participation.

The beauty of the fanzine is its glorious range. You can, and should, make a zine about your favorite band or TV show. But the definition of "fan" can be as broad as your imagination. I've seen a fanzine dedicated entirely to brutalist architecture in Eastern Europe, complete with stark black-and-white photos and historical notes. I once bought a tiny, pocket-sized zine that was a loving tribute to the humble garden snail. It had delicate illustrations, facts about snail biology, and a poem about their silvery trails. The creator wasn't just a biologist; she was a fan of snails. She saw the magic in something slow, slimy, and overlooked, and she wanted to share that magic with the world.

Think back to your brain dump list. What's that one thing you can talk about for hours, the thing that makes your friends' eyes glaze over but lights you up inside? That's your fanzine. It could be a deep-dive analysis of a single film, a collection of recipes from a fantasy novel, a fashion zine dedicated to a specific historical era, or a tribute to a local basketball player. It's a space for your uncool, hyper-specific obsession to be treated with the seriousness and passion it deserves.

Making a fanzine is an act of celebration. It's taking your love for something and transforming it into a tangible object, a sermon for the unconverted. You get to be the critic, the historian, the artist, and the cheerleader all at once. You are building a tiny monument to something you love, and in the process, you send up a flare to all the other people who love it, too.

Comp Zines: Making Something Better, Together

There's a persistent myth of the artist as a solitary genius, toiling away alone in a dusty attic. Zines can certainly be a solo project, but some of the most exciting and vibrant zines are born from community. This is the world of the compilation, or "comp," zine. Think of it less like writing a novel and more like hosting a potluck. You provide the theme and the venue, and everyone else brings a dish.

The process is simple and beautiful. You, the editor, pick a theme. The theme can be concrete, like "Cats of Instagram," or abstract, like "The feeling of Deja Vu." You then put out a call for submissions online or within your local community. You might ask for a single page of art, a 200-word story, a poem, a comic, a photo—whatever fits the theme. As the submissions roll in, your job is to curate them, arranging them into a cohesive whole before printing and stapling.

The result is a chorus of voices instead of a solo. I once contributed to a comp zine on the theme of "Public Transportation." My page was a short, grumpy poem about a crowded bus. Next to it was a beautiful, intricate drawing of a subway map. A few pages later was a deeply personal story about a conversation overheard on a train. No single one of us could have captured the entire experience of public transit, but together, our twenty different perspectives created a rich, multifaceted portrait. The final zine was so much more than the sum of its parts.

Organizing a comp zine is also a fantastic way to dip your toes into zine-making if you're feeling overwhelmed. The pressure isn't solely on you to generate all the content. Your role shifts from creator to curator, which is a different but equally creative skill. It's an act of community-building. You're providing a platform for others, forging connections, and creating a time capsule of what a specific group of people were thinking and feeling about a certain topic at a certain moment in time.

Informational & How-To Zines: Share Your Skills and Knowledge

You are an expert. Read that again. You are an expert. Maybe you're not an expert in quantum physics or Renaissance literature, but you are absolutely an expert in something. And that expertise is the seed of an informational or how-to zine. This genre is rooted in the punk and DIY ethos of skill-sharing, of empowering people to do things for themselves rather than relying on corporations or inaccessible institutions.

The first how-to zine I ever treasured was called Fix Your Bike. It was crudely drawn, with smudged fingerprints on the pages, but its instructions on how to patch a tire were clearer and more useful than any official manual I'd ever seen. The author wasn't a certified mechanic; they were just a person who knew how to fix a bike and wanted to share that freedom with others. That's the spirit of the how-to zine. It democratizes knowledge.

Look at your brain dump list again. What's on there that you know how to do? Maybe you have a foolproof method for making cold brew coffee. That's a zine. Maybe you know how to identify three local edible weeds. That's a zine. Maybe you have a system for organizing your digital files, a guide to thrift store shopping in your city, or a set of tips for dealing with social anxiety at parties. All of those are incredibly valuable informational zines waiting to be made.

These zines don't have to be dry or boring. In fact, they're better when they're not. Inject your personality into it. Add doodles, personal stories, and jokes. An informational zine about wild mushrooms is good; an informational zine about wild mushrooms that includes the story of that one time you thought you found a chanterelle but it was a poisonous look-alike is great. Your expertise isn't just the facts you know; it's the experience you have. Share it. You never know whose life you'll make easier, or more interesting, with the knowledge you take for granted.

Artistic Principle: Finding Your Unique Voice and Niche

We've explored the what—perzines, fanzines, comps, how-tos. But the final, magical ingredient is the you. There might be a thousand zines about cats, but there is only one potential zine about cats from your unique perspective. This is where we talk about voice and niche, two words that sound like they belong in a marketing meeting but are actually at the heart of all meaningful art.

Your 'voice' isn't something you decide on one day. You don't just pick 'witty and sarcastic' or 'earnest and poetic' from a list. Your voice is the natural, unavoidable result of your entire existence. It's the sum of the books you've read, the music you love, your weird sense of humor, your private heartbreaks, the way you talk to your best friend, and the things that make you angry. It's not about trying to sound like someone else; it's about getting quiet enough to hear how you already sound.

Making zines is the best practice for developing that voice. With each zine, you get a little closer to it. My first zines were a clumsy imitation of the Riot Grrrl zines I admired. They were full of righteous anger that felt a bit performative because I was still figuring out what my own anger looked and sounded like. It wasn't until the silly ramen zine that I stumbled upon a part of my real voice: a little bit obsessive, a little bit funny, and deeply affectionate about small, mundane things. Your voice is discovered in the making.

And that voice is what creates your 'niche.' In zines, a niche isn't a target demographic; it's a signal of authenticity. A zine about 'gardening' is broad and forgettable. A zine about 'container gardening on a shady apartment fire escape using only recycled materials'—that's a niche. It's specific. It's born from real-life constraints and experience. It speaks directly to a small group of people who have that exact same problem, and it feels like a gift just for them. Your niche is found at the intersection of your passions and your particulars. It's what you love, filtered through the unique lens of your life. Lean into your quirks. Celebrate your limitations. Combine your disparate interests. A zine about baking and punk rock? A zine about urban planning and ghost stories? Yes. That's where the magic is. That's your niche.

So, what's your zine about? It's about that weird thing on your brain dump list that you were almost too embarrassed to write down. It's about that memory that keeps popping up. It's about that one thing you love so much you could talk about it for hours. It doesn't need to be a 'Good Idea.' It just needs to be your idea.

Pick one. Just one thing from that beautiful, messy map of your mind. Pick the one that makes your heart beat a little faster, whether with excitement or with fear. That's it. That's the one. Now go get your scissors. It's time to start.

The Zinester's Toolkit: A Treasure Hunt for Supplies

Okay, so you're standing at the edge of the diving board. You've shaken off the fear of the blank page, you've got a head full of buzzing, beautiful, and maybe slightly weird ideas. The revolutionary spirit is there. The only thing missing is… well, everything else. The actual stuff. Before your brain can trick you into thinking you need a professional design studio and a small business loan to get started, let's reframe this entire process. This isn't a shopping list. It's a treasure hunt. It's an adventure in seeing the world not for what it is, but for what it could become in your hands.

Your first zine-making kit won't be found in the pristine aisles of a big-box art supply store. It will be assembled. It will be scavenged. It will be born from desk drawers, recycling bins, and the forgotten corners of your house. My first toolkit was a chaotic jumble: a half-dried-up glue stick, a pair of scissors I'd had since elementary school with my name written on the handle in fading marker, a stack of printer paper I'd "borrowed" from my dad's home office, and a handful of magazines my mom was about to throw out. It wasn't glamorous, but it was everything I needed. The act of gathering these humble materials is your first creative decision. It's where the zine truly begins.

The Holy Trinity: Paper, Scissors, and a Glue Stick

Let's boil it down to the absolute, non-negotiable essentials. If you have paper, something to cut it with, and something to stick it together with, you can make a zine. Full stop. This is the sacred, unbreakable foundation of zine-making. It's the punk rock three-chord progression of self-publishing. You don't need anything else to start. I once made a mini-zine on a long bus ride using only the back of a folded-up flyer, a tiny pair of nail scissors from my bag, and a glue stick I bought for a dollar at a pharmacy during a rest stop. It was crude, it was messy, and it felt completely and utterly magical.

Embracing this minimalism is liberating. It strips away all excuses. You can't say, "I can't start until I buy a better printer," or "I need to get some fancy pens." No, you don't. You need paper, scissors, and glue. The simplicity forces you to focus on the one thing that truly matters: your idea. Your voice. The message you want to put out into the world. The constraints of these three simple tools can ignite a firestorm of creativity. When your options are limited, you have to get clever. You learn to tear paper in interesting ways, to use negative space, to create texture with just a few simple folds.

Think of these three items as your permission slip. They grant you the authority to create without judgment. A crookedly cut image? That's style. A visible glue mark? That's texture. A slightly misaligned page? That's character. This isn't about achieving a sterile, machine-made perfection. It's about leaving your human fingerprints all over your work. The Holy Trinity isn't just a set of tools; it's a philosophy. It's a declaration that you have everything you need to begin, right here, right now.

Paper Deep Dive: Weight, Texture, and Finding Freebies

Once you've embraced the basic trio, you can start playing with the ingredients. And paper, my friend, is where the real fun begins. That idea of the zine as a "tactile rebellion" starts here. The feel of the paper is the first handshake your zine gives its reader. A standard sheet of 20-pound copy paper is the default, the blank canvas. It's cheap, it's accessible, and it folds beautifully. It's the reliable workhorse of the zine world, and there's absolutely no shame in it. Most of the zines I've made and loved are printed on this very paper.

But the world is full of paper, and most of it is free if you know where to look. This is where your treasure-hunting skills come into play. Start seeing the world as a potential paper source. Junk mail is a goldmine. The weirdly patterned insides of security envelopes make for incredible collage backgrounds. Glossy real estate flyers offer vibrant blocks of color. Discarded office memos, printed on only one side, give you a clean slate with a history. Old, yellowed book pages have a built-in sense of nostalgia and gravitas. Even brown paper bags have a wonderful, rustic texture.

Pay attention to weight and texture. A heavier paper, like cardstock, makes for a sturdy, durable cover that feels substantial in the reader's hands. It says, "This is an object to be kept." A thin, almost transparent paper, like tracing paper or onion skin, can be used for overlays, creating layers of text and image that interact in fascinating ways. Construction paper, with its rough, toothy surface, grabs ink and pencil differently than smooth copy paper. Every choice communicates something. A zine made entirely of found and recycled paper tells a story of resourcefulness and environmental consciousness before the reader even deciphers a single word.

Cutting Tools: Beyond Basic Scissors (X-Acto Knives, Rotary Cutters, and Safety)

Your trusty pair of scissors will get you far. They are perfect for rough-and-tumble collages and cutting out big, bold shapes. But as you get deeper into zine-making, you might find yourself craving a little more precision. This is when you graduate to the more specialized tools in the cutting family. The X-Acto knife, or craft knife, is the scalpel of the collage artist. It allows for an incredible level of detail—cutting out intricate patterns, slicing out the space between a subject's arm and their body, or creating delicate windows in a page.

Using an X-Acto knife feels different. It's less about hacking away and more about drawing a line with a blade. It requires a steady hand and a bit of patience, but the results are sharp and clean in a way scissors can never be. Always, always use it with a self-healing cutting mat underneath. I learned this the hard way, leaving a permanent scar on the surface of a beautiful wooden desk I'd salvaged. That scar was a good teacher. Which brings me to the most important part of using a craft knife: respect the blade. Always cut away from your body, keep your fingers clear of the blade's path, and replace blades when they get dull. A dull blade is far more dangerous than a sharp one because it requires more pressure, increasing the chance of a slip.

Then there's the rotary cutter. It looks like a tiny pizza cutter and it's the secret to perfectly straight, clean edges. Paired with a metal ruler, a rotary cutter glides through paper, creating flawless lines for trimming the edges of your finished zine or cutting multiple pages to the exact same size. It's a tool of satisfying efficiency. While an X-Acto knife is for delicate surgery, a rotary cutter is for swift, decisive action. You don't need these tools, but knowing what they do opens up new possibilities for how your finished zine can look and feel.

Adhesives 101: Choosing the Right Glue for the Job (and Avoiding Wrinkles)

If you've ever tried to make a collage with a bottle of white school glue, you know the heartbreak of the wrinkled page. You place your perfectly cut-out image, smooth it down, and come back an hour later to find a warped, buckled mess. Choosing the right adhesive is a quiet art, but it's one that will save you endless frustration. Your best friend, and the undisputed champion of zine-making, is the humble glue stick.

Glue sticks are a dry adhesive, meaning they have very low moisture content. This is key. They provide a solid bond without soaking into the paper and causing those dreaded wrinkles. They are forgiving, cheap, and portable. A good rule of thumb is to apply the glue to the back of the smaller piece you're sticking down, rather than directly onto your master page. This gives you more control and prevents excess glue from smudging your layout. Get a few. Keep one in your bag. You never know when a zine idea will strike.

For more advanced techniques, you might explore rubber cement. This was a revelation for me. Rubber cement allows for a temporary bond. You can coat the back of an image, let it dry, and then position it on your page. It remains tacky enough to stay put, but you can still lift it and move it around until you get the placement just right. Once you're happy, you put a second coat on the master page, press the two together, and it creates a permanent bond. Any excess cement can be rubbed away with your finger or a special rubber cement pickup tool. It's the secret weapon for perfectionists who want to experiment with layout without full commitment.

Other glues have their place, but should be used with caution. A thin line of PVA or craft glue can be great for binding a spine, but it's generally too wet for collage work. Double-sided tape is another fantastic, no-mess option for creating clean, flat bonds. The point is to think about what you're trying to achieve. Do you need a quick, permanent bond? Glue stick. Do you need to reposition things? Rubber cement. Are you adding a heavy object like a piece of fabric or cardboard? Maybe a stronger, wetter glue is needed, but apply it sparingly.

Sourcing Your Visuals: Magazines, Old Books, Junk Mail, and Public Domain Archives

Your zine is a conversation, and collage is how you invite other voices into the discussion. Sourcing images is one of the most joyful parts of the process. It's a form of visual poetry, of finding meaning in the discarded and overlooked. Magazines are the classic starting point. Ask friends, family, doctor's offices, and libraries if they have old issues they're getting rid of. Each type of magazine has its own visual language. Old National Geographics are filled with stunning nature photography and portraits from around the world. Vintage fashion magazines offer elegant figures and bold typography. Tabloids provide wonderfully absurd headlines and grainy, dramatic photos.

Don't stop at magazines. Old books, especially textbooks and encyclopedias from thrift stores, are a treasure trove of diagrams, maps, and illustrations. A high school biology textbook can give you anatomical drawings; a 1950s home economics book can provide surreal images of domestic bliss. Junk mail, as I mentioned, is fantastic for corporate logos, sterile stock photos, and urgent-looking text. By taking these images out of their original context, you strip them of their power to sell or persuade and give them a new life and a new meaning in your own work.

And we live in a magical time where the digital world offers another, impossibly vast archive. Websites hosting public domain images are your best friend. The Library of Congress, the New York Public Library Digital Collections, Wikimedia Commons, and the Public Domain Review are bottomless pits of historical photos, scientific illustrations, weird advertisements, and medieval manuscripts. You can lose hours, even days, just falling down these rabbit holes. You can print these images out and incorporate them into your physical zine, creating a bridge between the past and the present, the analog and the digital. The key is to always be looking, always be collecting. Create a folder or a box where you stash interesting images. You're building your visual vocabulary.

Writing & Drawing Tools: Pens, Markers, Typewriters, and More

The visuals may set the mood, but your words and marks are the heart of the message. The tool you use to write or draw with is as much a part of your voice as the words themselves. A simple ballpoint pen is honest and direct. A fine-tipped black Micron pen creates clean, consistent lines that are perfect for detailed drawings or neat handwriting. A thick, chisel-tipped

Sharpie is loud, bold, and unapologetic. It screams from the page.

Experiment with different tools to see how they feel. Paint markers can give you opaque, vibrant color on any surface, even dark paper or over a photograph. Highlighters, often dismissed as a mere study tool, can be used to create blocks of transparent color. Pencils offer a softness and the ability to smudge and blend, giving your pages a more intimate, sketchbook-like feel. Don't feel like you need to be a masterful artist. Stick figures can be just as powerful as photorealistic portraits if they serve your story. The wobbly, imperfect quality of a hand-drawn line is part of the charm.

And then, there's the typewriter. If you can get your hands on one—from a thrift store, a flea market, or a grandparent's attic—you will discover a whole new way of writing. Each letter is a physical act, a hammer striking paper through ink. The clack-clack-clack is a rhythm, a soundtrack to your thoughts. There is no delete key. A mistake is either crossed out with a string of X's or embraced as part of the text's history. This forces a certain kind of mindfulness. Typewritten text has an immediate and undeniable aesthetic. It feels official and yet deeply personal, a dispatch from another time that is perfectly at home in the world of zines.

The 'Nice-to-Have' Box: Stamps, Washi Tape, Stickers, and Other Embellishments

If the previous sections cover the essentials—the flour, water, and salt of your creative kitchen—this section is the spice rack. These are the things that add flair, personality, and unexpected moments of joy. I keep a shoebox on my desk that I call my "bits box." It's filled with all the little odds and ends that might one day find a home in a zine.

Inside, you'll find rolls of washi tape, the colorful, semi-transparent Japanese paper tape that's perfect for creating borders, holding down photos with a decorative touch, or just adding a splash of pattern. There are sheets of stickers—the gold-star kind from a teacher supply store, glittery ones from a vending machine, and address labels I can write or draw on. Rubber stamps are another fantastic tool. You can buy them or, for the truly dedicated, carve your own out of erasers to create custom logos or repeating motifs.

This box also contains things like thread and a needle for hand-sewing the binding instead of stapling it, old postage stamps, bus tickets, dried flowers, pieces of fabric, and security envelopes I've saved. This is the stuff that makes your zine uniquely yours. It's a collection of textures and memories. Don't feel pressured to buy any of this. Simply start your own bits box. The next time you see a cool-looking candy wrapper, a strangely beautiful receipt, or a fallen leaf, save it. You're not hoarding; you're curating your future palette.

As you stand back and look at your assembled collection—the scavenged papers, the trusty scissors, the half-used glue stick, the box of colorful bits—you'll realize something important. The treasure hunt wasn't just about finding supplies. It was about changing how you see the world. A pile of junk mail is now a stack of possibilities. A boring office supply is now a tool for revolution. You've already started. You've gathered your materials, and in doing so, you've gathered your courage. Now, let's put them to use.

The Classic 8-Page Mini: Your First Zine, From a Single Sheet of Paper

Welcome to your first, and perhaps most magical, hands-on project. In the world of zines, there is no form more iconic, more accessible, or more instantly gratifying than the 8-page mini. This is the quintessential zinester's handshake, a tiny marvel of paper engineering that transforms a single, standard sheet of paper into a complete, pocket-sized booklet with a front cover, a back cover, and six internal pages. There's no glue, no staples, no complex binding—just a series of clever folds and one strategic cut. This chapter is a self-contained workshop designed to guide you from a blank page to a finished, tangible zine in your hands. We will banish the fear of the blank page and the intimidation of complex projects. Today, you are not just learning a technique; you are creating a finished product. By the end of this chapter, you will hold your very first zine, a testament to your creativity and a passport into the vibrant world of self-publishing.

Project Overview: Making the Quintessential One-Page Foldable Zine

The 8-page mini-zine, sometimes called a one-page wonder or a pocket zine, is the perfect entry point for any aspiring creator. Its beauty lies in its constraints and its simplicity. You don't need a fancy studio or expensive supplies. All you need to complete this project is a single sheet of standard letter-sized (8.5" x 11") or A4 paper, a pair of scissors, and something to write or draw with. That's it. The goal of this project is to demystify the process of creation and give you a tangible win. You will learn the physical process of folding and cutting the zine, but more importantly, you will learn how to think within the structure of a booklet—how to plan a beginning, a middle, and an end across its eight small pages.

This format is beloved by zinesters for its versatility. It's perfect for short stories, a collection of poems, a mini-comic, a personal manifesto, a how-to guide, a recipe, or a showcase for a few favorite drawings. Its small size makes it unintimidating to fill, and its low-cost production (just the price of a photocopy) makes it incredibly easy to share, trade, and distribute. Before we begin, take a moment to appreciate the potential held within your single sheet of paper. It is a flat, two-dimensional object that, with a bit of paper-folding alchemy, will soon gain a third dimension and a narrative structure. It's time to make some magic.

Step 1: The Magic Fold (A Visual, Step-by-Step Guide with Diagrams)

This is a purely physical process, so put your pens down for a moment. Find a flat surface. We will describe each fold as if you were looking at a diagram. For the best results, make every crease as sharp and precise as possible. Run your thumbnail or the edge of a ruler over each fold to set it firmly. Fold 1: The 'Hot Dog' Fold. Take your sheet of paper and place it in front of you in 'portrait' orientation (the shorter sides are at the top and bottom). Now, fold it in half lengthwise, bringing the right edge over to meet the left edge perfectly. Crease it down. When you are done, you should have a long, skinny rectangle. Unfold it. You now have a central crease running down the middle of your paper.

Fold 2: The 'Hamburger' Fold. Now, turn your paper to 'landscape' orientation (the longer sides are at the top and bottom). Fold it in half, bringing the top edge down to meet the bottom edge. Crease it firmly. Don't unfold it this time. You should now have a rectangle that is half the original size.

Fold 3: The Final Panel Folds. With your paper still folded in half from the previous step, take the top flap and fold it back up, bringing its edge to meet the top folded edge you just created. Crease it. Now, flip the entire paper over. Do the same thing on this side: take the new top flap and fold it back up to meet the central folded edge. Crease it firmly. You should now have a smaller, thicker rectangle that has been folded into an accordion or 'W' shape when viewed from the side. Unfold your paper completely. You should see eight rectangular panels marked out by your crease lines. You've just created the grid for your zine!

Step 2: Making the All-Important Cut

This step is the only time you'll need your scissors, and it's what turns your folded grid into a collapsible book. It might feel a little nerve-wracking the first time, but it's quite simple. First, take your paper, which should be fully unfolded to show the eight panels. Fold it in half again using the 'hamburger' fold (landscape orientation, folding the top edge down to the bottom). The folded edge should be at the top, and the two open edges should be at the bottom.

Now, identify the central crease line. It runs from the middle of the folded top edge down to the open bottom edge. You are going to cut along this line, but DO NOT cut all the way through. You will cut only from the folded edge to the next horizontal crease line—the one that marks the center of the paper. In other words, you are cutting along the spine of the two middle panels. Your cut should start at the center of the folded edge and stop at the T-junction where the creases meet. You are essentially cutting a slit into the very heart of your paper.

When you are done, unfold your paper. It should be a full sheet again, but now with a gaping 'mouth' in the middle. This is exactly what you want! This single, precise cut is the secret to the entire construction. It allows the paper to pivot and collapse into book form. Hold it up to the light and admire your handiwork. The hard part is over.

Step 3: Planning Your 8 Pages (Front/Back Cover, Spreads, and Page Flow)

This is where your brain has to do a little flip. The layout of the pages on the flat sheet is not intuitive. Before you put a single permanent mark on your paper, it's critical to understand which panel corresponds to which page, and in what orientation. We highly recommend doing this with a light pencil first. Take your unfolded, cut sheet and lay it in landscape orientation. You will see two rows of four panels each. The bottom row of panels will be upside down relative to the top row when it's folded into a book. This is the most common point of confusion, so let's map it out explicitly.

The page layout on the flat sheet is as follows, viewed in landscape orientation. Top Row (from left to right): - Page 7 - Page 6 - Page 5 - Page 4 Bottom Row (from left to right, all panels are upside down): - Page 8 (back cover) - Page 3 - Page 2 - Page 1 (front cover) For clarity, the bottom row of panels must be created upside down. The bottom-right panel is the front cover (Page 1).

The panels to its left are Page 2 and Page 3, with the bottom-left panel being the back cover (Page 8). The top row of panels is oriented right-side up. From right to left, they are Page 4, Page 5, Page 6, and Page 7. To ensure correct orientation, lightly number each panel in a corner with a pencil and include an arrow to indicate the 'up' direction for that panel.

Now that you have it mapped, you can start thinking like a zine-maker. Page 1 is your cover—it needs a title and maybe a key image. Page 8 is your back cover, perfect for your name, contact info, or a concluding thought. Pages 4 and 5 form the center spread; this is a great place for a larger drawing or a piece of text that spans two pages. The other pages (2, 3, 6, 7) are your content, and you must consider the flow. What does the reader see when they turn from page 1 to 2? What's the cliffhanger on page 3 that makes them want to see the center spread? Planning this flow is the key to a zine that feels cohesive and intentional.

Step 4: Let's Fill It In! A Guided Creative Session to Beat the Blank Page

The blank page is a zinester's greatest foe. Let's defeat it together with a simple, guided theme: 'A Tour of My Desk.' It's a subject you are an expert on, it's immediately available, and it's more interesting than you think. Keep your zine flat for now while you fill it in. Grab your favorite pen or marker. Page 1 (Front Cover - remember, bottom right, upside down!): Give it a title. Something simple like "On My Desk" or "The World of My Workspace." Add your name as the author. Draw a picture of your favorite object on your desk: a coffee mug, a cool pen, a sleeping cat.

Page 2 (Bottom row, second from right, upside down): This is your introduction. Write a short sentence or two. "Welcome to my desk. It's a place of chaos and creation." Draw a little map of your desk layout from a bird's-eye view. Page 3 (Bottom row, third from right, upside down): Focus on one object. The computer or laptop. Write a short sentence about it. "My window to the world (and endless distractions)." Draw a simplified icon of a computer screen.

Pages 4 & 5 (The Center Spread - top row, right and center-right, right-side up): This is your big feature! Choose 2-3 interesting objects and draw them across the two pages. A stack of books, your collection of pens, a plant. Label them. For example: "Item A: Unfinished novels." "Item B: Pens that may or may not work." "Item C: A plant I'm trying not to kill." Page 6 (Top row, second from left, right-side up): Let's talk about sound. What do you hear at your desk? The clicking of keys, music, the hum of the fan? Write "Sounds of the space:" and list a few. Add some musical notes or 'zzz's for a quiet space.

Page 7 (Top row, far left, right-side up): The conclusion. What's one thing you'd add to your desk if you could? "Future addition: a dedicated snack drawer." Or a concluding thought: "This mess is where the magic happens." Page 8 (Back Cover - bottom row, far left, upside down): Time to sign off. Write "Made by [Your Name] on [Date]." You can add your social media handle, a tiny self-portrait, or just a big "The End." Now, take a step back. Your flat sheet is filled with content. It might look like a strange, disjointed map of ideas, but it's about to become a book.

Troubleshooting: 'My Folds are Wonky!' and Other Common Frustrations

Even the simplest creations can have their frustrating moments. Don't worry, every zinester has been here. Let's solve some common problems. Problem: My final folded zine is puffy and the pages don't line up. This is almost always an issue with the initial creases. Sharp creases are everything. When you first fold your 8-panel grid, go back over every single fold and press it down hard with a thumbnail, the back of a spoon, or a bone folder if you have one. A crisp fold holds its shape; a soft fold fights back. It's worth re-folding your paper to sharpen the creases before you try to collapse it.

Problem: I cut in the wrong place / I cut all the way across the paper! Congratulations, you have performed the most common rite of passage in 8-page-zine making! There is no fixing this. But the good news is, you've only wasted one sheet of paper. Take a deep breath, grab a new sheet, and see it as a practice run. This time, you'll be extra careful to only cut along that single, central panel line.

Problem: It won't collapse into a book! It's just a weird paper shape. This is the final, slightly tricky step of assembly. After creating your content, fold the paper in half lengthwise (the 'hot dog' fold). You should have a long strip with the 'mouth' you cut in the middle. Now, hold the two ends and gently push them towards the center. The cut 'mouth' will open up, and the paper should naturally form a plus-sign or star shape. Once you have that plus-sign shape, simply choose one panel to be the front cover and fold the other pages behind it, collapsing the star into a neat little book. The final page should fold around to become the back cover. The central fold of the book is formed by the creases you made, not the cut edge.

Problem: I drew my pages upside down! Another classic! This is why we pencil in the numbers and orientation arrows first. If it's too late, you have two options: embrace it as a quirky, experimental zine, or start over. Remember, making mistakes is a huge part of learning the craft. Every 'ruined' zine is a lesson learned for the next one, which will be even better.

You Did It! Admiring and Sharing Your First Creation

Go ahead and perform the final collapse. Push the ends together, form the star, and fold it into a booklet. Give it one last firm press. Now, hold it in your hand. Feel the weight of it. Flip through the pages, from your front cover to your back cover. Read it. You did that. You took a blank, flat object and imbued it with ideas, art, and structure. You transformed it into a vehicle for a message, a tiny portable world that you created from scratch.

This is a moment to celebrate. Don't rush past it. The feeling of holding your first finished zine is powerful. It proves that you can have an idea and see it through to a physical conclusion. It silences the inner critic that says making things is too hard or requires special skills. You just did it with paper, scissors, and a pen. This little book is your proof.

So, what now? Share it! The entire culture of zines is built on sharing. Show it to a friend or family member. Read it to your pet. Leave it on a coffee shop table for a stranger to find. The true magic happens when your creation makes a connection with someone else. And if you want to make more copies, you don't need to re-draw it. Simply unfold your master copy and place it on a photocopier. For the price of a few cents, you can create a whole edition to trade, sell, or give away. You are no longer just a reader or a consumer of me-

dia; you are a creator, a publisher, a zinester. Welcome to the club.

The Art of the Page: Composition, Collage, and Visual Storytelling

Welcome to the heart of the zine-making process. If previous chapters were about finding your voice and gathering your materials, this chapter is about giving that voice a physical form. A zine page is more than just a container for words or a frame for a picture; it's a stage, a playground, a miniature gallery. It's where your ideas stop being abstract and become tangible artifacts that someone can hold, look at, and connect with. We're moving beyond what you want to say and diving deep into how you want to say it, visually. This is the art of composition—the deliberate, playful, and sometimes chaotic arrangement of elements to create meaning, emotion, and rhythm. Forget the intimidating specter of 'Graphic Design.' We're here to get our hands dirty with paper, glue, and ink, and to learn how to turn a blank page into a compelling visual story.

In this chapter, we'll demystify the core principles of layout and design, translating them into the practical, accessible language of the cut-and-paste creator. We'll explore how to make images and text talk to each other, how to build a mood with collage, and how to create stunning lettering even if you can't draw a straight line. Most importantly, we'll learn to embrace the unique aesthetic of the handmade, finding beauty in imperfection and power in authenticity. Prepare to think of your zine not just as a collection of pages, but as a series of visual experiences.

Artistic Principle: Thinking in Spreads, Not Just Pages

One of the most significant shifts you can make as a zine creator is to stop seeing individual pages and start seeing 'spreads.' A spread is a set of two facing pages that a reader views simultaneously when a booklet is open. Think about it: unless it's the very first or very last page, no page is ever seen in isolation. Page 2 is always next to page 3. Page 4 is always next to page 5. These two pages are in a constant conversation, and you, the creator, are the moderator.

This simple realization opens up a universe of creative possibilities. Instead of designing one page at a time, you can design the entire visual field. A large photograph can stretch across the center fold (the 'gutter'), uniting the two pages into a single, panoramic canvas. A line of text can begin on the left page and conclude on the right, pulling the reader's eye across the divide. You can create powerful visual dynamics through contrast: make the left page dense, chaotic, and full of text, while the right page features a single, tiny image floating in a sea of white space. The resulting tension is palpable and deliberate.

To put this into practice, lay out your master copy flat, showing all the spreads. Use your thumbnail sketches from the planning phase. How does the end of one page lead into the beginning of the next?

Can a visual element from page 3 'bleed' over to page 4? Can you create a rhythm where a series of busy spreads is followed by a quiet, contemplative one? Thinking in spreads elevates your zine from a simple collection of information to a choreographed experience, guiding your reader's journey with intention and flair.

Technique Spotlight: Found Poetry and Text-Based Collage

Words are not just carriers of meaning; they are visual objects. The shapes of letters, the weight of a font, the texture of the paper they're printed on—all of these are artistic materials waiting to be used. Found poetry and text-based collage are techniques that celebrate this dual nature of text, allowing you to build pages that are as visually fascinating as they are meaningful.

Found poetry is the art of creating a poem by 'finding' words and phrases in an existing text. Your sources are everywhere:

old, discarded books, science textbooks, glossy magazines, newspapers, instruction manuals, and junk mail. The process is a treasure hunt. Scan the text not for its original meaning, but for words that leap out at you. Cut these words or phrases out. Now, working on a blank page, arrange them. Don't think about grammar or sense at first; focus on rhythm and association. 'The forgotten sky,' 'a mechanical heart,' 'whispers only.' You are a linguistic sculptor, chipping away the unnecessary to reveal a new form.

This technique inherently creates a rich visual collage. The mix of fonts, sizes, and paper colors from your various sources builds a textured, layered background. You can arrange your found words into neat lines, scatter them like confetti, or spiral them around a central image. This is a powerful way to overcome writer's block. You aren't starting from a blank page; you are remixing the world around you. It's an act of deconstruction and reconstruction, taking the mundane language of everyday life and transforming it into something personal and poetic. Let the visual character of the words themselves guide your composition.

Working with Images: Creating a Mood and Narrative Through Pictures

Images in a zine are never just decoration. They are co-storytellers, working with (or sometimes against) your text to build a world for the reader. The images you choose, and how you present them, are your primary tools for setting the mood, establishing a narrative, and creating an emotional impact. Your image library is limitless: family photos, magazine clippings, illustrations from old encyclopedias, your own drawings, photocopied textures, postcards, or stills from films.

One of the most potent collage techniques is juxtaposition. By placing two seemingly unrelated images next to each other, you create a third, invisible meaning in the space between them. A picture of an astronaut next to a picture of an ant creates a story about scale, ambition, or loneliness. A vintage advertisement for a housewife next to an image of a wolf creates a narrative of hidden wildness. Don't just look for images that literally illustrate your text; look for ones that add a new layer of irony, emotion, or mystery.

Play with scale and cropping to command the viewer's attention. Take a tiny object, like a button, and photocopy it at 400% until it becomes a monstrous, abstract circle. Take a huge landscape and crop it down to a tiny, intriguing square of texture. Repetition is another powerful tool. Using the same image multiple times on a page can create a hypnotic pattern, show the passage of time, or emphasize a feeling of being overwhelmed or obsessed. Remember that the quality of the image is also a choice. A grainy, high-contrast photocopy feels urgent and raw, while a glossy, full-color magazine image feels slick and commercial. Use these qualities to your advantage to tell the story you want to tell.

Layout Fundamentals: Grids, Margins, and White Space (Yes, Even in a 'Messy' Zine!)

The words 'grid' and 'margin' might conjure images of rigid, corporate design, but in the world of zines, they are your secret weapons for creating pages that feel intentional, even when they're bursting with chaotic energy. These are not rules to be followed, but tools to be understood and then used—or broken—with purpose.

Margins are the empty borders around the edges of your page. They act as a frame, containing your content and preventing it from feeling like it's about to fall off the paper. Even a thin, wobbly, hand-drawn margin tells the reader's brain, 'The art happens inside this line.' It gives the eye a place to rest and makes the content feel more focused. Without margins, a page can feel stressful and hard to read.

A grid is just an underlying structure that helps you organize your content. It doesn't have to be a complex matrix of intersecting lines. A simple grid for a zine page could be a single line drawn down the middle, creating two columns. Or it could be three horizontal bands. You can create these guides by lightly folding your paper or drawing faint pencil lines. This structure helps you align elements, creating a sense of order that makes even the most eclectic collection of images and text feel cohesive. Once you have that underlying order, you can then choose to have elements 'break' the grid for dramatic effect, making the moment of chaos feel deliberate.

Finally, let's talk about white space (or negative space). This is the most powerful and misunderstood tool in design. White space is not 'empty' space. It is active, breathing room for your content. A page crammed from edge to edge with no white space is visually shouting. It can be effective for creating a sense of anxiety or information overload, but it's exhausting for the reader. By contrast, placing a single small word or image in the center of a mostly blank page makes that element feel incredibly important and profound.

White space directs the eye, creates emphasis, and provides moments of quiet in the visual noise. Don't be afraid of empty; it's where your content gets its power.

Hand-Lettering for Non-Artists: Simple Tricks for Great-Looking Text

Let's get one thing straight: you do not need 'good handwriting' to create amazing hand-lettering for your zine. In fact, slick, perfect calligraphy can sometimes feel out of place in a raw, handmade publication. Your unique, quirky, and personal handwriting is part of your voice. This section is about giving you simple, repeatable tricks to make your text feel intentional, dynamic, and visually engaging, no matter your skill level.

One of the easiest and most effective techniques is 'faux calligraphy.' Write your title or headline in your normal cursive handwriting. Now, go back and look at each letter. Every time your pen made a downward stroke, thicken that line. That's it. This simple act of adding weight to the downstrokes instantly transforms your regular cursive into something that looks elegant and stylized.

For a bolder look, try block letters. Instead of trying to draw the letter in one go, construct it. Lightly sketch out the basic shapes of the letters, almost like you're building them out of sticks. Then, draw the outline around your skeleton sketch. You now have hollow letters you can fill in with color, pattern, or leave empty. To add dimension, draw a simple drop shadow: just draw a second outline of the letter, slightly offset down and to one side, and fill it in. Instant 3D effect!

Don't underestimate the power of your tools. Write the same word three times: once with a thick chisel-tip marker, once with a leaky ballpoint pen, and once with a fine-liner. The character of the text changes dramatically. The tool does the work for you. You can also trace fonts you like from magazines or computer printouts, or use simple stencils (a bottle cap makes a perfect 'O'). The key is to treat lettering as drawing. It's about making interesting shapes, not achieving perfect penmanship. Play, experiment, and find the styles that feel like you.

Combining Words and Images: The Push and Pull of a Good Layout

This is where all the pieces come together. A great zine page isn't just about having interesting words and interesting images; it's about the dynamic interplay between them. How do they interact? How do they guide the reader's eye? How do they combine to create a meaning that is greater than the sum of their parts? This relationship is a dance, and you are the choreographer.

Start by establishing a clear visual hierarchy. Not everything on the page can be equally important. One element needs to be the star of the show. This is your dominant element—it could be a large, compelling photograph, a bold, hand-lettered headline, or an expansive block of text. This is the first thing the reader's eye should be drawn to. Everything else on the page should play a supporting role, arranged in a way that complements the dominant element without competing with it. This creates a clear entry point for the reader and prevents the page from feeling like a jumbled mess.

Think about the physical interaction between your text and images. Don't just place them next to each other in boring blocks. Let them touch! You can have your text wrap tightly around the contour of a cut-out image, creating a beautiful organic shape. You can print your text directly on top of a low-contrast photograph, making the image a textured background. You can have an image physically interrupt a column of text, forcing the reader to jump over it. Each of these choices creates a different feeling. Wrapping text feels harmonious, while interrupting it feels more abrupt and energetic.

Most importantly, consider the narrative relationship. Do your words explain your image? Does your image illustrate your words? Or do they create a tension by contradicting each other? A photo of a beautiful, serene beach paired with text about an ecological disaster is far more powerful than a photo of an oil spill. This push and pull, this harmony and dissonance between what we see and what we read, is the engine of compelling visual storytelling. It's the space where you invite the reader to think, question, and feel.

Embracing Imperfection: The Wabi-Sabi of Cut-and-Paste Aesthetics

We live in a digital world saturated with pixel-perfect graphics, flawless airbrushing, and clean, vectorized lines. The cut-and-paste zine stands in beautiful, defiant opposition to this slickness. Its power lies in its very imperfection. To truly master the art of the page, you must learn to embrace—and even celebrate—the happy accidents, the smudges, and the crooked lines.

There is a Japanese aesthetic philosophy called wabi-sabi, which centers on finding beauty in imperfection, imperma-nence, and authenticity. A wabi-sabi ob-ject is cherished not in spite of its flaws, but because of them. This is the perfect mindset for a zine maker. The visible glue stain on the edge of a picture, the slightly tilted line of text, the grainy texture from a tenth-generation photocopy—these are not mistakes. They are evidence of the human hand. They are proof that a real person, with their own unique quirks and limita-tions, made this object. They are markers of authenticity.

When you allow yourself to let go of perfection, you unlock a new level of cre-ative freedom. You stop being paralyzed by the fear of 'messing up' the blank page. You can work faster, more intuitively, and more honestly. A torn edge has more char-acter than a perfectly cut one. The texture of layered paper, with its bumps and shad-ows, has a depth that a flat digital image can never replicate. The slight misalign-ment of a photocopied page gives it a vi-brating energy.

So, let your lines be wobbly. Let your glue show. Embrace the grit and grain of the photocopier. In a world of sterile perfection, the handmade, imperfect object feels real, warm, and inviting. It is a testament to the beauty of the process and the value of your unique, human touch. Your zine's 'flaws' are its soul. Don't hide them; put them on display.

Putting It All Together: Assembling Your Master for Copying

You've done it. After hours spent with scissors, a trusty glue stick, and a typewriter or your favorite pen, you have a pile of finished pages. They're spread across your floor or desk, a beautiful mosaic of your hard work and weird ideas. There's the cover you're so proud of, that collage that came together like magic, the hand-lettered title that took three tries to get right. It's a powerful moment, looking at all the pieces of your story laid out like that. But there's a quiet, slightly panicked question that follows: How does this pile of paper become a booklet?

This is the part of the process that can feel like a daunting final exam in some arcane subject you never signed up for. It's the bridge between your one-of-a-kind creation and the stack of multiples you'll soon be trading, selling, or leaving in coffee shops. This chapter is all about building that bridge. We're going to take your individual, finished pages and assemble them into a 'master copy'—the sacred original you'll take to the photocopier. It's a technical process, yes, but it's also a kind of magic. It's the final, loving act of craft that turns your vision into a reproducible reality.

What is a 'Master Copy' and Why Does It Matter?

In the simplest terms, your master copy is the original, camera-ready version of your zine, laid out on flat sheets of paper exactly as they need to be fed into a photocopier. It's not a bound booklet. Instead, it's a series of single sheets of paper, each containing two or more pages of your zine, arranged in a very specific, and often counterintuitive, order. This is the version you will guard with your life on the way to the copy shop.

Why does it matter so much? Because the photocopier is a machine of pure repetition. It has no artistic sensibility. It will reproduce exactly what you give it, flaws and all. That faint pencil line you forgot to erase? It will be on every copy. That cat hair stuck under a piece of tape? It will be immortalized in black toner one hundred times over. That shadowy mark from a glob of wet glue? It will become an unintentional part of your design.

Your master copy is your one chance to get everything perfect. It's the blueprint. The quality of your entire print run rests on the quality of these few original sheets. A clean, crisp, and correctly formatted master is the difference between a stack of professional-looking zines and a pile of expensive, frustrating mistakes. This isn't about being a perfectionist in a world that celebrates messy creativity; it's about respecting your own work enough to present it clearly. Your ideas deserve to be seen without the distraction of smudges and shadows.

Understanding Pagination and Imposition (The Page Puzzle)

Here it is. The single most confusing concept for almost every first-time zinester. You have your pages numbered 1, 2, 3, 4, and so on. Your brain logically wants to put them in that order. But when you're creating a master for a folded booklet, logic gets turned on its head. This is the world of imposition, and it's a delightful little puzzle.

Imposition is the art of arranging your zine pages on the master sheets so that when they are printed, folded, and assembled, they appear in the correct numerical order. For example, in a standard 8-page zine made from a single sheet of paper (like the mini-zine from Chapter 5, but scaled up), the front cover (page 1) will often be on the same flat sheet as the back cover (page 8). The second page might sit next to the seventh page. It feels wrong, but it's completely right.

The best way to wrap your head around this is to stop thinking of your zine as a stack of single pages and start thinking of it as a series of folded spreads. Take a few sheets of paper, fold them in half to make a little blank booklet, and staple the spine. Now, number the pages. Start with '1' on the front cover, '2' on the first inside page, and so on until you get to the back cover. When you're done, carefully remove the staple and unfold the pages. Look at the flat sheets. See how the numbers are arranged? That's your imposition map. Page 2 is opposite the second-to-last page. The centerfold pages are right next to each other. This is the secret code you need to follow.

Imposition Cheat Sheet: Printable Templates for Common Zine Formats (Quarter-size, Half-size)

While making your own numbered dummy is the best way to learn, you don't have to reinvent the wheel every time. For common zine sizes, you can create standardized templates that become your indispensable guides for assembly. These aren't complicated digital files; they are physical sheets of paper that serve as your map.

For a quarter-size zine (a standard 8.5x11" sheet folded into 8 pages), your template is one piece of paper. You'll fold it into eighths, number the pages as a booklet, and then unfold it. On this unfolded sheet, you'll clearly write the page numbers in their correct positions. You'll see, for instance, that page 8 and page 1 are on one end, and page 4 and page 5 are in the middle, upside down relative to the others. This single sheet is your cheat sheet. When you're pasting up your master, you'll place this template next to you and arrange your finished content onto a fresh, clean sheet of paper, matching this layout exactly.

For a half-size zine (made from 8.5x11" sheets folded in half, like a program), your page count will be a multiple of four (8, 12, 16, 20 pages, etc.). Your master copy will consist of several sheets, each printed on the front and back. For a 12-page zine, for example, you'll have three sheets of paper. Your imposition puzzle involves figuring out which pages go on which sheet. The outermost sheet will contain pages 1, 2, 11, and 12. The next sheet will hold pages 3, 4, 9, and 10. The center sheet will have pages 5, 6, 7, and 8. Creating a numbered, stapled dummy booklet is non-negotiable for this format. It is the only way to be certain your pages are in the right place before you commit with glue.

Technique Spotlight: The 'Pasting Up'
Process for Clean, Sharp Copies

With your imposition map figured out, the mechanical part begins. 'Pasting up' is the old-school graphic design term for the physical act of gluing down your finished elements—text blocks, images, drawings—onto your master pages. This is where your zine finally takes its finished form, just before it hits the copier. This is the moment of commitment.

You'll need a clean, well-lit workspace, your master sheets (the number depends on your zine format), your finished content elements, a good glue stick, a ruler, and maybe a craft knife or paper cutter for final trims. Work on one master sheet at a time. For a quarter-size zine, you have one large sheet to fill. For a half-size, you'll have several sheets, each with a 'front' and a 'back' side.

Lay down your blank master sheet. Using your imposition template or dummy zine as a guide, start placing your content. Place the artwork for page 1 in the box marked '1'. Place the artwork for page 8 in the box marked '8'. Use a ruler to make sure things are straight. Check that you have enough margin around the edges so nothing gets cut off during printing or trimming. Once you're happy with the placement, carefully apply glue to the back of your content element—edge to edge!—and press it down firmly onto the master sheet. Smooth it out from the center to eliminate air bubbles. Repeat this for every single page. It's a slow, methodical process. It's a meditation. It's the last time your hands will build this specific object.

Tips for a Good Master: Avoiding Glue Globs, Shadow Lines, and Crooked Pages

The road to a beautiful stack of zines is paved with the ghosts of bad master copies. I've made them all. I once spent $40 copying a zine only to discover that a huge, shadowy blob appeared on page 5 of every copy. The culprit? A massive glob of cheap, wet glue that had soaked through the paper of my master, creating a translucent spot that the photocopier dutifully interpreted as a gray smudge. It was a painful, expensive lesson.

Your best defense is a high-quality, acid-free glue stick. It provides a strong hold without the wetness that causes wrinkling and those dreaded shadow lines. Apply a thin, even coat. If you're pasting a small element onto a larger page, it's sometimes better to paste the entire page onto a new, clean sheet of paper. This ensures there are no raised edges from your collage pieces that could cast shadows under the strong light of the copier.

Crooked pages are another common pitfall. Our eyes can deceive us. Use a ruler and a T-square if you have one. Lightly draw guidelines with a pencil (a non-photo blue pencil is even better, as most copiers won't see it) to align your text blocks and images. Align the top of your content with your guideline, not the bottom. It creates a more visually pleasing and consistent look. And after you've glued something down, hold the master sheet up to a bright light or a window. This will instantly reveal any hidden glue smears, fingerprints, or pieces of dust that need to be cleaned up before you head to the copy shop.

Making a 'Flat Plan' or Dummy Zine to Guide Your Layout

I cannot overstate the importance of this one little trick. Before you ever touch your final artwork or a glue stick, you should create a 'dummy zine.' This is your zine in miniature, a rough draft that serves as your guide for both content flow and technical assembly. It is your single greatest tool for preventing costly mistakes and layout headaches.

Take the exact number of sheets you'll be using for your final zine, fold and staple them into a blank booklet. This is your dummy. Now, with a pencil, sketch out the entire zine. Don't worry about making it pretty. Just write 'COVER ART HERE' on the front. On page 2, write 'Introduction text.' On pages 3-4, 'Photo spread.' On page 5, 'Poem,' and so on. Go through the entire booklet.

This simple act does two crucial things. First, it allows you to feel the pacing of your zine. You can flip through it and see if that big article feels too long, or if a blank page might be more powerful next to a dense collage. You can catch awkward page turns—like the punchline of a comic being revealed before you turn the page. Second, once you're happy with the flow, this dummy becomes your imposition guide. You can take it apart, unfold the pages, and you have the exact map for how to lay out your master copy. It removes all the guesswork and replaces it with certainty.

Final Pre-Flight Check: Proofreading and Reviewing Your Master Before You Copy

Your master pages are complete. They are clean, straight, and correctly imposed. You're ready. But before you run out the door, giddy with excitement, there is one final, critical ritual: the pre-flight check.

This is your last chance to catch any errors before they are multiplied by 20, 50, or 100.

First, proofread everything one last time. And I mean everything. Page numbers, your contact info, every caption, every sentence. The best way to do this is to read it aloud. Your ear will catch awkward phrasing and typos that your eyes have become blind to. Better yet, have a friend read it. A fresh set of eyes is an invaluable asset. I once printed 75 copies of a zine about my favorite band before noticing I had misspelled the lead singer's name on the cover. The feeling is... not good.

Next, do a technical review. Are all the page numbers there and in the right order? Double-check against your dummy. Is anything too close to the edge of the paper? This is the 'trim area,' and anything in it risks being sliced off. Are all the pages facing the right direction? (This is especially important for quarter-size zines where some pages are upside down on the master). Hold each sheet up to the light one last time. Look for any smudges, eraser marks, or stray hairs. This is your moment of final quality control. Taking ten minutes for this check can save you an hour of regret and a wallet full of wasted cash.

When you're done, you'll be holding more than just a few sheets of paper. You'll be holding the culmination of your entire creative process. All the brainstorming, writing, drawing, and collaging has led to this: a tangible, reproducible artifact. It's the ghost of the zine that is about to be born. It feels solid, finished, and full of potential. The hard part is over. Now, for the magic.

The Ghost in the Machine: Creating Zines with Digital Tools

For the last seven chapters, we've been living in a beautifully messy, analog world. We've celebrated the tactile joy of paper, the satisfying snip of scissors, and the unforgiving permanence of a glued-down image. We've romanticized the smudge of a typewriter key and the charming imperfection of a crookedly stapled spine. So, I can feel your hesitation from here. A chapter on digital tools? Isn't that a betrayal of the whole ethos? Doesn't inviting the computer to the party feel like inviting a slick, corporate executive to a punk show?

I get it. I really do. For years, I was a staunch purist. My zines were proudly, almost defiantly, analog. To me, the computer represented everything zines were fighting against: sterility, perfection, and a lack of soul. But one day, I was working on a zine with a very specific, repeating background pattern I wanted. I tried hand-drawing it, but my hand cramped and the inconsistencies drove me mad. I tried making a stamp, but it was blotchy. Frustrated, I opened a basic drawing program on my laptop, created the pattern in ten minutes, printed it out, and then proceeded to collage and write all over it by hand. It was a revelation. The computer wasn't the enemy; it was just another tool in the box. A very, very powerful one.

This chapter isn't about replacing your glue stick with a graphics tablet. It's about expanding your creative arsenal. It's about finding the ghost in the machine—the human touch, the creative spark, the messy soul—within the clean and ordered world of pixels. It's about learning how to make the computer work for your vision, not the other way around.

Why Go Digital? The Pros and Cons of Pixels vs. Paper

The decision to incorporate digital tools is less a philosophical stand and more a practical choice, project by project. Thinking about it as a rigid binary of "analog versus digital" is a trap. The real magic happens when you see them as collaborators. But before we dive in, it's worth being honest about what you gain and what you might lose when you move from the physical desktop to the digital one.

The most seductive whisper from the digital world is a single command: Undo. Anyone who has ever painstakingly placed a tiny piece of collage only to realize it's crooked, or worse, covering up essential text, knows the heart-sinking finality of dried glue. The digital undo button is a safety net, a time machine, a quiet reassurance that experimentation doesn't have to be terrifying. Beyond that, digital tools offer unparalleled precision. You can align text boxes perfectly, resize images without a trip to the photocopier's zoom function, and ensure your margins are consistent on every single page. This control can be liberating, especially for text-heavy zines or those with a clean, minimalist aesthetic.

On the other hand, something vital can get lost in translation. The analog process is full of what I call "happy accidents." A smear of ink, a crinkle in the paper from too much glue, an image that gets slightly distorted on the photocopier—these imperfections give a zine its unique texture and life. They are physical evidence of the creator's hand. A purely digital workflow can sometimes feel too clean, too perfect. It's easier to fall into a generic, template-driven look if you're not careful. The screen can feel cold and distant compared to the immediate, tangible feedback of paper under your fingertips. There's a physical conversation that happens when you make things by hand, a dance between your intention and the material's properties, that is harder to replicate with a mouse and keyboard.

The resolution to this debate isn't choosing a side. It's realizing that you don't have to. The most exciting path for many zinesters today lies in the space between these two worlds.

Simple Zine Layout in Free Software (Canva, Google Slides)

You don't need a fancy, expensive subscription to a professional design suite to start making zines on a computer. In fact, some of the most accessible tools are ones you might already use for work presentations or creating social media graphics. Let's demystify this. Think of a program like Canva or even Google Slides not as complex software, but as a clean, digital desk with an infinite supply of paper, text, and images.

The first step is to set up your digital "paper." In any of these programs, you can create a custom page size. If you're making a standard half-letter zine (an 8.5x11 inch sheet folded in half), you'd set your page dimensions to 5.5 inches wide by 8.5 inches tall. Instantly, you have a digital canvas that matches the final page of your physical zine. This simple act makes the whole process feel less intimidating and more connected to the end product you'll hold in your hands.

From there, you can start building your pages. Text boxes behave like little strips of paper you've typed on and are moving around the page. You can try out dozens of fonts in seconds, something that would require a massive typewriter collection in the analog world. You can upload your own photos or drawings and drag them into place, resizing and rotating them with a click. It's a digital form of collage, offering a level of flexibility that a glue stick can only dream of. The key is to approach it with the same playful, experimental mindset as you would a physical page. Don't get bogged down in the endless options; use the tools to quickly bring your core idea to life.

For the Artists: Using Procreate, Krita, or Photoshop for Zine Pages

If you're an illustrator or someone who loves to draw, digital art software like Procreate (for iPad), Krita (a fantastic free and open-source option), or Adobe Photoshop can completely transform your zine-making process. These programs move beyond simple layout and into the realm of pure creation, allowing you to craft entire pages from scratch with a depth and versatility that's hard to match.

The concept of layers is the single biggest game-changer. With traditional media on a physical page, adding a solid color background after a character is drawn requires painstakingly painting around it. If you then add text, you have to be careful not to write over your character. In a program like Procreate, each of these elements can exist on its own transparent sheet. This allows for a layer for a pencil sketch, one on top for final ink lines, another beneath it for color, and a separate one at the very top for text. You can change the background color without affecting your drawing and move text around without smudging the ink. It's like having an infinitely editable stack of tracing paper, providing the freedom to build complex, multi-element pages without fear.

Furthermore, the world of digital brushes is a universe in itself. You can find or create brushes that perfectly mimic the texture of charcoal, the watery bleed of watercolor, the sharp line of a technical pen, or the gritty spray of an aerosol can. You can bring a rich, analog-feeling texture to your work while still benefiting from the editability of a digital format. For artists, this means you can create your comic panels, illustrations, or hand-lettered titles with incredible control, knowing that each element can be tweaked, resized, or recolored until it's just right.

The Hybrid Method: The Best of Both Worlds

Here is where the real fun begins. The hybrid method throws the "pixels versus paper" debate out the window entirely. It acknowledges the strengths of both realms and encourages you to move fluidly between them. This is not about compromise; it's about synergy. It's about using digital tools for what they do best—precision, repetition, and editing—and using analog methods for what they do best—texture, spontaneity, and soul.

Combining Digital Layouts with Analog Collage and Textures

One of my favorite hybrid techniques starts with the computer. I'll design the core of my zine pages in a simple layout program. I'll set up the columns of text, place any digital photos, and get the basic structure exactly how I want it. I'll ensure the alignment is perfect and the fonts are crisp and readable. Then, I hit print. This printed page is not the final product; it's my canvas.

With this structured, digitally-created base, I can now get my hands dirty. I'll attack it with my analog tools. I might add hand-drawn borders around the clean text boxes. I'll glue on scraps of textured paper, fabric, or cut-outs from magazines. I might add a watercolor wash over a section, letting it bleed into the printed text. I might even spill a little coffee on it and let it dry to create an aged effect. Once this new, multi-layered, and beautifully messy page is complete, this becomes my master copy for the photocopier. The final zine has the best of both worlds: the legibility and structure of digital design, and the warmth, texture, and undeniable human touch of handmade art.

Scanning Your Analog Art to Use in Digital Layouts

This approach flips the process on its head. It begins in the physical world. You make your art the old-fashioned way: a beautiful ink drawing, a complex cut-and-paste collage on a piece of cardboard, a painting, a page of handwritten poetry. You create these elements without the constraint of a screen, focusing purely on the physical craft. When you're done, you take these artifacts to a scanner.

The scanner is a portal, a magical bridge that transports your physical creations into the digital realm. Watching your hand-drawn lines or carefully glued collage appear on the screen is a small miracle. Once digitized, these elements become incredibly flexible. You can take that single ink drawing and duplicate it, resize it, or layer it over a digital photograph. You can scan a piece of textured paper you made and use it as a background for your entire zine. You can take a snippet of handwriting and place it precisely next to a block of typed text. This method allows you to retain the raw, organic quality of your analog work while giving you the powerful compositional tools of a digital layout program to assemble your final pages.

Finding Digital Collage Fodder: Public Domain Archives and Digital Ephemera

Remember the treasure hunt for collage materials we talked about in Chapter 4? The thrill of sifting through old magazines, junk mail, and forgotten books? That same adventure exists online, and the archives are infinitely larger. When you're working digitally, you have access to a staggering amount of visual material, much of it free to use, remix, and reimagine.

Your first stop should be the world of public domain archives. These are vast online collections of images, documents, and illustrations whose copyrights have expired, making them free for all to use. Websites like The Public Domain Review, the Library of Congress Digital Collections, the New York Public Library Digital Collections, and the Flickr Commons are digital goldmines. They are the internet's equivalent of a dusty, sprawling antique store filled with wonders. You can get lost for hours, stumbling upon medieval astronomical charts, 19th-century botanical illustrations, bizarre diagrams from old patent filings, and stark, beautiful photographs from a hundred years ago. Downloading one of these images and dropping it into your zine layout feels like collaborating with history itself.

Beyond these formal archives, think about the digital ephemera of your own life. That weirdly cropped screenshot from a video call, a glitchy image from a corrupted file, a photo of the texture of your cat's fur, a meme that perfectly encapsulates a feeling. These are your modern-day found objects. They can be integrated into your zine to give it a contemporary, personal feel that is just as authentic as a scrap of paper from an old magazine. The treasure hunt is the same; only the terrain has changed.

Preparing Your Digital File for Printing

So you've designed your pages on the computer. They look beautiful on your screen, a perfect collection of individual artworks. Now comes the final puzzle, the digital equivalent of creating the master copy we discussed in the last chapter: preparing your file for the printer. This is where you translate your creative vision into a technical reality that a print shop—or your own home printer—can understand.

The most important concept to grasp here is imposition, which we touched on before. It's the art of arranging your zine pages in the correct order for printing. If you just send a file with pages 1, 2, 3, 4 in order, the printer will spit out single sheets. For a booklet, you need to arrange them in 'printer spreads'. Remember our trusted paper dummy? The logic is identical. For an 8-page zine, you need a PDF file where page 1 is next to page 8, page 2 is next to page 7, and so on. Many design programs have booklet-making functions that can do this for you, but you can also do it manually by creating a new, larger document (11x8.5 inches for a standard zine) and placing your finished pages in the correct spots. Always, always print a single test copy and fold it to make sure your pages are in the right place and orientation before you print fifty of them.

Two other technical details will save you from heartbreak. First is resolution, measured in DPI (dots per inch). For printing, your images and file should be at least 300 DPI. Anything lower, especially images grabbed from the web, will look blurry and pixelated on paper. Second, export your final, imposed file as a PDF. A PDF (Portable Document Format) is a universal file type that locks everything in place. It ensures that the fonts you chose, the placement of your images, and the layout you perfected will look exactly the same on the print shop's computer as it does on yours. It's the digital equivalent of handing over a perfectly prepared master copy.

An Introduction to E-Zines and PDF Zines

So far, we've talked about using digital tools to create a physical object. But what if the zine itself never touches paper? What if its final form is purely digital? Welcome to the world of e-zines and PDF zines, a parallel universe of zine-making where distribution is instant and global, and printing costs are zero.

An e-zine is simply a zine designed to be read on a screen—a computer, a tablet, a phone. Most commonly, these are distributed as PDFs. This format opens up a completely new set of creative possibilities.

Since you're not limited by the mechanics of printing and binding, you can play with format in exciting ways. Your zine can be in full, vibrant color without costing you a fortune at the copy shop. More excitingly, you can embed hyperlinks. A line in your perzine about a band you love can link directly to their music. A review of a movie can link to its trailer. Your zine can become a gateway, a curated portal to other parts of the internet.

Of course, there is a trade-off. You lose the tactile experience. No one will ever feel the paper of your e-zine, smell the ink, or put it on a shelf. It's a different kind of artifact. It's not better or worse, just different. For many creators, the ability to share their work with someone on the other side of the world with a single click is a powerful motivator. It's a way to participate in the global conversation instantly, another evolution of the zinester's core mission: to get your voice out there, by any means necessary.

Ultimately, the tools don't define the zine. The spirit does. The ghost in the machine is you—your ideas, your passion, your unique way of seeing the world. Whether you wield a glue stick or a stylus, a typewriter or a keyboard, you are participating in that same secret war against silence that began with sci-fi fans and their mimeograph machines. The machine has changed, but the ghost—the urgent, human need to create and connect—remains exactly the same.

The Magic of the Photocopier: Printing, Folding, and Binding

For weeks, maybe months, your zine has been a singular, precious object. It's a stack of master pages on your desk, a fragile collage of paper and glue, or a pristine set of files on your computer. It exists only for you. This is the quiet, intimate phase of creation. But zines are not meant to be solitary creatures. Their true purpose, their soul, is found in multiplicity. They are meant to be copied, shared, traded, left on bus seats, and discovered in the corners of record stores. And that transformation from a single object into a potential army of ideas happens in one place: the photocopier.

This is the moment of truth, the industrial heartbeat that brings your zine to life. If previous chapters were about finding and shaping your voice, this one is about giving it an echo. We're stepping out of the cozy chaos of your creative space and into the bright, humming world of the copy shop. It can feel like a final exam, a place where your messy, heartfelt creation meets the cold, hard reality of machinery. But I want you to reframe that. The photocopier isn't a judge; it's a magical amplifier. It's the tool that turns your whisper into a chorus.

Befriending Your Local Copy Shop: How to Talk to the Pros

I remember my first time walking into a copy shop with my master pages. I felt like I was smuggling contraband. The pages were a mess of glued-on text, white-out, and slightly crooked images. I clutched the folder to my chest, convinced the person behind the counter would laugh me out of the store. He was a guy named Dave who looked profoundly bored, and when I nervously explained I wanted to make "a little booklet," he just nodded, took my pages, and said, "Saddle-stitched? How many?"

He wasn't a critic; he was a technician. He was, in his own way, a collaborator.

The person behind the counter at your local print and copy place is your single greatest ally in this process. They have seen it all, from slick corporate reports to frantic last-minute school projects. Your weird little zine is not going to shock them. More importantly, they understand their machines better than you ever will. They know which machine produces the richest blacks, which one handles cardstock without jamming, and how to wrangle the settings to get the best results from a less-than-perfect master copy. Don't be afraid to ask for their help.

Instead of just handing over your pages and hoping for the best, start a conversation. Say something like, "Hey, I'm printing my first zine. The master copy has a lot of photo collage and some text. What's the best way to copy this so the dark areas are really dark but the text doesn't get blurry?" This shows you respect their expertise. Always, always ask for a single test copy first. This allows you to check for errors in your imposition (are the pages in the right order?), see how the contrast looks, and make sure nothing got cut off. It's much cheaper to fix a mistake on one copy than on fifty.

Photocopier Settings to Know and Love: Contrast, Paper Size, and Double-Sided Printing

While the pro at the copy shop is your guide, understanding the basic language of the machine empowers you. You're the artist; these settings are your new paintbrushes. The most important setting, the one that defines the classic zine aesthetic, is contrast. A photocopier works by seeing the world in black and white. Turning up the contrast makes light areas lighter and dark areas darker. This is the secret to that iconic, gritty, high-contrast look.

For collages made from old magazines or grayscale photos, cranking up the contrast can blow out the subtle mid-tones, turning a soft gray into a stark black or a brilliant white. This isn't a flaw; it's a feature. It unifies disparate elements and gives your pages a bold, graphic quality. For hand-drawn line art, it makes your lines crisp and sharp. Experiment with it. A test copy with normal contrast versus one with high contrast will immediately show you the aesthetic power you hold. Sometimes, you might even want lower contrast to preserve the delicate texture of a pencil drawing.

The other critical settings are more straightforward but just as important. You'll need to specify the paper size you're printing on—usually standard letter (8.5x11 inches) or legal (8.5x14 inches) for most zines that will be folded in half. Then there's the question of double-sided printing. If you've laid out your master copy correctly (as we discussed in Chapter 7), you'll have one sheet for the front and back of your pages. You need to tell the machine (or the person operating it) to print on both sides of the paper. Pay close attention to the orientation—how the machine flips the page. Most have an option to flip on the "long edge" or "short edge." For a standard booklet, you'll almost always want to flip on the long edge to ensure your pages aren't upside down relative to each other.

Let's Talk Paper: Choosing the Right Stock for Your Covers and Interior Pages

The feel of the paper is the first handshake your zine gives its reader. Before they even read a word, they will feel its weight, its texture, its sturdiness or its fragility. Your choice of paper stock is not just a technical detail; it's a crucial part of the zine's personality. The most common and affordable option is standard 20 lb bond paper—the stuff you find in any office printer. It's cheap, it's reliable, and it's perfectly fine. A zine printed on this paper feels immediate, ephemeral, and authentically DIY.

But you have other options. Stepping up to a slightly heavier 24 lb or 28 lb paper for the interior pages can make a world of difference. The zine feels more substantial, and there's less "show-through," where you can see the printing from the other side of

the page. This can be especially important if your zine is heavy on dark images or
bold text.

Where you can really make a statement
is with the cover. Using a heavier paper,
known as cardstock (typically 65 lb or even
80 lb), gives your zine a protective shell and
a professional feel. It makes it stand out in
a stack of other zines. And this is where
you can play with color. Even if your entire
zine is printed in black and white, printing it on colored paper, or just printing the
cover on colored cardstock, can completely change its mood. A punk zine might feel
right at home on bright yellow or neon
pink paper. A quiet poetry zine might be
perfect on a muted gray or cream stock.
The color isn't just decoration; it sets the
emotional tone.

The Zen of Collating, Folding, and Stapling

You've returned from the copy shop with a
stack of flat, double-sided sheets. It doesn't

look like a zine yet. It's a pile of potential. Now comes the final, physical, and often deeply meditative part of the process: assembly. If your zine is more than one sheet of paper, your first task is collating. This simply means arranging the pages in the correct order for each individual zine. If your zine has three sheets (Sheet 1: pages 1, 2, 11, 12; Sheet 2: pages 3, 4, 9, 10; etc.), you'll create stacks, each containing one of each sheet in the right sequence.

Clear a large table or a patch of floor. Put on some music. This is your personal assembly line. The repetition can be incredibly calming. As you fold each zine, you are the first person to experience it as a booklet. You'll see your spreads come together for the first time. You'll notice how one page flows into the next. Each fold is an act of creation, transforming a flat sheet into a three-dimensional object with a beginning, a middle, and an end. Be precise with your folds. A crisp, clean fold along the centerline makes the zine sit flat and look professional. Align the corners carefully before running your finger or a bone folder along the spine to make the crease sharp.

This is also your last chance for quality control. As you handle each copy, you might notice a printing error, a smudge, or a page that's slightly crooked. You can set these aside. This hands-on process connects you to every single copy of your work. You aren't just mass-producing an object; you are personally finishing a small batch of art, and your touch is the final ingredient.

Binding Technique: The Classic Saddle-Stitch (Two Staples, Long-Arm Stapler)

The most common, efficient, and iconic method for binding a zine is the saddle-stitch. That's just a fancy term for "stapling along the spine." For a standard zine folded in half, this means two staples along the fold. If you try to do this with a regular desktop stapler, you'll quickly run into a problem: the stapler's arm isn't long enough to reach the middle of the page.

You'll end up with a mangled, frustrating mess.

Enter the zinester's secret weapon: the long-arm stapler (also called a long-reach stapler). It's exactly what it sounds like—a stapler with an extended base and arm that allows it to easily reach the center of a folded sheet of paper. They are an affordable and incredibly worthwhile investment if you plan to make more than one zine in your life. To use it, you open your folded zine and lay it face down, so the cover is on the table. You position the stapler so the arm is along the spine, and place one staple about an inch or two from the top, and another an inch or two from the bottom. The result is a clean, secure, and professional-looking binding that allows the zine to open flat.

A pro-tip for a cleaner finish: After stapling, close the zine and place it on a self-healing cutting mat or a thick piece of cardboard. Take a metal spoon and firmly rub the back of it over the staples on the outside of the spine. This flattens the staples, making them less likely to snag and giving your zine a more polished feel.

Binding Technique: Hand-Sewn Binding (The 3-Hole Pamphlet Stitch)

If the saddle-stitch is the efficient workhorse of zine binding, hand-sewing is the artisanal poet. It takes a little more time, but it adds an unmistakable touch of craft and care. The most common and easiest method is the 3-hole pamphlet stitch. All you need is a needle, some sturdy thread (waxed linen thread is ideal, but embroidery floss or even dental floss can work in a pinch), and an awl or a pushpin to poke the holes.

First, with your zine folded, use a ruler to mark three points along the spine: one in the exact center, and one each about an inch from the top and bottom. Use your awl to poke a hole through all the pages at each mark. Now, for the sewing. Cut a piece of thread that is about three times the height of your zine. Starting from the outside of the zine, push your threaded needle through the center hole, leaving a tail of a few inches on the outside. Go from the inside up through the top hole, then all the way down the outside to the bottom hole. Go through the bottom hole to the inside, and finally, bring the needle back out through the center hole.

You should now have both ends of your thread on the outside of the spine, on either side of the long stitch that runs from top to bottom. Simply tie a secure square knot around that long stitch, trim the ends, and you're done. The result is a beautiful, durable binding that literally stitches your story together. It tells the reader that every part of this object was made with intention, right down to the thread holding it together.

How Many to Print? Calculating Your First Print Run Without Breaking the Bank

This is the final, terrifyingly practical question. You're standing at the copy shop counter, your test print is perfect, and Dave asks, "So, how many?" Your answer depends less on math and more on intention. Why did you make this zine? Who is it for?

If this is a perzine about a very specific personal experience, and you just want to share it with your ten closest friends, then print fifteen. Give one to each friend and keep a few for your archive. The cost will be minimal, and the purpose will be perfectly fulfilled. If you made a fanzine about your favorite obscure band and you're going to their concert next month, maybe a print run of 50 is the right call. You can hand them out to fellow fans in line, making new friends and sharing your passion. If you're preparing for your first zine fest, 50 to 100 copies is a common starting point. It's enough to fill your table and have plenty to sell or trade, but not so many that you're stuck with boxes of them if it doesn't sell as well as you hoped.

Remember the economics of photocopying: the price per copy often goes down the more you print. It might only cost a few cents less per zine to print 100 instead of 50, but that adds up. Ask for a price breakdown. But don't let a bulk discount tempt you into printing 500 copies of your very first zine. Start small. It is a far greater feeling to sell out of a small print run and have to make more than it is to have four giant boxes of unsold zines gathering dust in your closet for the next decade. You can always print more later. That's the beauty of this whole process.

And so, you walk out of the copy shop, not with a fragile master copy, but with a stack of solid, real, finished zines. Or perhaps you're sitting on your living room floor, a long-arm stapler at your side, surrounded by neatly folded booklets. The magic is complete. Your voice, your art, your weird ideas—they are no longer confined to your head or your desk. They are now objects in the world, ready for their journey. Each one is a handshake, a secret message, a potential connection waiting to be made. You did it. You didn't just make a zine; you made zines. Plural. And in that plurality, all the power lies.

Get It Out There! Sharing Your Zine and Finding Your Community

There's a strange, quiet moment that comes after the whir of the photocopier has faded and the last staple has been punched. You're sitting on your floor, surrounded not by one singular, precious master copy, but by a family. A stack of twenty, fifty, maybe a hundred identical little booklets, all born from your brain and your hands. They have that fresh, slightly warm smell of toner and paper. They exist. They are real.

For so long, the challenge was internal. It was about finding your voice, wrestling with ideas, and conquering the physical process of creation. But now, a new kind of silence descends, and it asks a different, more exhilarating question: So... now what? That stack of zines on your desk is a pile of potential conversations. They are dormant. Their true purpose, the very soul of the zine ethos, is not just to exist but to travel, to be held by other hands, to be read by other eyes. Your monologue is finished; it's time to invite others into the dialogue. This chapter is about that leap—the moment your zine leaves home and finds its people.

Zine Culture is Sharing Culture: The Joy of the Trade

Before we even whisper the word "selling," we have to talk about the real currency of the zine world: other zines. The foundational act of zine community is the trade. It's a transaction rooted not in commerce but in mutual admiration and a shared secret. It's the embodiment of the punk rock, anti-capitalist spirit that has fueled this medium for decades. Saying, "I'll trade you my zine for your zine," is one of the most beautiful sentences in the English language.

I remember my first trade with excruciating clarity. I was at a small punk show, clutching a few copies of my very first, very embarrassing perzine about feeling alienated in my hometown. I saw someone else with a zine—a cool, hand-drawn comic about a girl and her ghost friend. I spent three full songs working up the courage to approach her. My hands were sweating. I probably mumbled something like, "Uh, I made this thing. It's not very good. Do you... wanna trade?" She just smiled, handed me her comic, and took mine. That was it.

Walking away with her zine in my hand felt like I had just completed a spy movie dead drop. It was a transfer of trust. She trusted me with her art, her story, and I trusted her with mine. Reading her zine later that night was a revelation. I wasn't just a consumer; I was a peer. The trade flattens hierarchies. It says that the thing you poured your heart into, no matter how messy or amateur, has the same inherent worth as the thing someone else poured their heart into. It is the purest form of connection in this entire subculture, a handshake that says, "I see you. I see what you made. And it matters."

Finding Your People: An Intro to Zine Fests, Fairs, and Swaps

If trading is the secret handshake, then a zine fest is the grand, joyous, wonderfully chaotic annual meeting of the secret society. The setting is typically a school gymnasium, a community hall, or a crowded bookstore basement, but instead of bake sales or sporting events, every table is overflowing with paper creations. Hundreds of zinesters sit behind tables piled high with their work: comics, perzines, political tracts, photo zines, recipe zines, and single-page poems. The air hums with the sound of flipping pages and excited chatter.

Your first zine fest as an attendee is a magical, overwhelming experience. You are suddenly, tangibly, surrounded by your people. These are the weirdos, the dreamers, the ranters, the poets who have also felt the pull to just make something. Walking through the aisles is like taking a tour through the collective unconscious of a city. You'll find a zine that perfectly articulates a feeling you thought only you had. You'll laugh at a comic that's so niche it feels like a personal joke. You'll buy a tiny, passionate zine about fungi or forgotten silent film stars, and you'll have a five-minute, deeply enthusiastic conversation with its creator.

And then, there's the next step: tabling at a fest yourself. This is it. This is your debut. Applying for a table can be intimidating, but most fests are incredibly welcoming to first-timers. The moment you finish setting up your little display—your stack of zines, maybe a handwritten sign—is terrifying and exhilarating. And then someone walks up, picks up your zine, and their face lights up. They hand you a few crumpled dollars or ask for a trade. In that moment, you are no longer just a person who made a thing. You are a zinester. You are part of the ecosystem. Finding your local or regional zine fest (a quick search online for "[Your City] Zine Fest" is usually all it takes) is the single most important step you can take to find your community in the physical world.

Selling Your Zine: Pricing, Platforms (Etsy, Big Cartel), and Packing Orders

Let's talk about money. It can feel... icky. After all this talk of community and trading, putting a price tag on your vulnerable little zine can feel like a betrayal. It isn't. Selling your zine isn't about getting rich; it's about sustainability. It's about recouping your printing costs so you can afford to make the next issue. It's about placing a small, tangible value on your time and labor, which is a radical act in itself.

So, how do you price it? There's no hard formula, but a good starting point is to calculate your cost-per-copy (total printing cost divided by the number of copies) and then add a little on top for your labor. If a zine cost you $1 to print, selling it for $3-$5 is perfectly reasonable. Remember, people aren't just paying for paper and staples; they're paying for your idea, your perspective, your art. Don't undervalue yourself. At the same time, zines are historically the art of the accessible. You're not trying to price people out. It's a delicate balance, but trust your gut.

When it comes to selling online, platforms like Etsy or Big Cartel are your friends. Etsy is a massive marketplace, which means a wider potential audience might stumble upon your work, but you're also a small fish in a giant ocean. Big Cartel is more streamlined and often favored by independent artists; it feels less like a mall and more like your own personal shop. Don't get paralyzed by the choice. Pick one that feels right and start there. The real magic happens after the sale.

Packing an order is another opportunity for connection. This isn't Amazon. You're not a robot dropping an item in a box. You're a person sending a piece of your soul to another person. Write a little thank-you note on a scrap of paper. Draw a smiley face on the envelope. Throw in a sticker or a button if you have one. This personal touch is everything. It's a reminder to the buyer that they are supporting an individual artist, and it transforms a simple purchase into a memorable experience. It's the digital equivalent of that smile and nod across a zine fest table.

Working with Zine Distros: How to Get Your Work Carried by Others

As you make more zines, you might start dreaming bigger than your own table or online shop. You might want your zine to reach people in cities you've never even visited. This is where zine distros come in. A distribution network, or "distro," is essentially a curated shop run by someone who lives and breathes zines. They act as a filter, a trusted voice who collects the best, most interesting zines they can find and presents them to a wider audience, either through an online store or by tabling at fests themselves.

Getting your zine into a distro is a huge vote of confidence. It means a respected member of the community saw your work and believed in it enough to champion it. The process usually involves finding a distro whose vibe matches your zine, and then following their submission guide-lines. This often means sending a polite email introducing yourself and your zine, along with a physical copy or a PDF for them to review. Be prepared for a "no," or even for no response at all. Distro owners are often one-person operations, flooded with submissions. Don't take it personally.

If they say yes, you'll typically work out a consignment deal. This means you send them a batch of your zines (say, 10 copies), and they pay you a percentage for each one that sells (often a 50/50 or 60/40 split in your favor). It's not a path to riches, but the feeling of seeing your zine listed on a beloved distro's website, nestled among the work of zinesters you admire, is a profound milestone. It means your voice is officially part of a larger chorus.

Leaving Your Zine 'In the Wild' (Guerilla Distribution and Public Art)

There is a deep, quiet magic in letting go. It's a method of distribution that asks for nothing in return and is perhaps the most aligned with the serendipitous spirit of zine discovery. This is the art of leaving your zine "in the wild." It's a form of guerrilla public art, a message in a bottle tossed into the sea of everyday life.

Think back to that record store where this whole journey began. Someone left that zine there. They didn't know who would find it. They received no money, no credit. They just trusted that it would find the right person. You can do the same. Leave a copy on a bus seat. Tuck it into the magazine rack at a laundromat. Slide it onto a shelf in the library, next to a book on a related topic. Leave one in a doctor's office waiting room. Abandon it on a table in a coffee shop.

Each zine you leave behind is a small act of creative defiance. It's an injection of the personal, the handmade, and the unexpected into a sterile, commercialized world. You will likely never know who finds it or what they think. But the act itself is the reward. You are creating a moment of potential discovery for a stranger, a tiny island of weirdness in their sea of sameness. You are paying forward the magic that you once received.

Building an Online Presence: Using Social Media to Connect with Readers and Other Zinesters

The zine world may have been born in an analog age, but it is thriving in the digital one. The internet, particularly visual platforms like Instagram, has become the zine community's sprawling, 24/7 common room. This isn't about becoming an "influencer." It's about connection. It's about finding the people who live too far away to meet at a fest and the zines you'd never find in your local distro.

Creating an account dedicated to your zine projects allows you to share your work, but more importantly, to share your process. Post a picture of a messy, in-progress collage. Share a snippet of text you're proud of. Talk about the frustrations of a printer jam. This authenticity is what draws people in. It's the digital equivalent of leaning over a zine fest table and saying, "This part took me forever to get right." Following hashtags like #zines, #perzine, #zinelife, or #zinefest will open up a live feed of what the community is making and talking about right now.

This is how you arrange trades with someone on the other side of the world. It's how you find out about online zine swaps or submission calls for collaborative zines. It's how you get a word of encouragement from another creator when you're feeling stuck. The goal isn't to broadcast, but to interact. Comment on other people's work. Ask questions. Share zines you've bought or traded for. Use your little corner of the internet to amplify other voices, and you'll find that the community will amplify yours in return.

Zine Etiquette: How to Be a Good, Supportive Community Member

Every subculture has its unwritten rules, a shared understanding that keeps the community healthy and supportive. The zine world is no different. It's a space built on mutual respect and a DIY ethos, and being a good citizen is just as important as making a good zine. These aren't commandments, but rather a friendly guide to navigating the social fabric of our wonderful world.

First and foremost: honor your trades. If you agree to trade zines with someone, send your zine. Life happens, delays occur, but ghosting on a trade is the zine world's cardinal sin. It breaks the chain of trust. Similarly, don't ask creators for free zines. Many zinesters operate on razor-thin margins or even at a loss. Buying their zine, even for a few dollars, is a direct and meaningful act of support. If they offer a freebie or a trade, that's different, but don't put them on the spot.

When you talk about other people's zines, focus on uplift. The culture is one of amplification, not criticism. If you read a zine you love, post about it. Tell your friends. Write a short, glowing review. But if you read a zine that isn't for you—especially a perzine, which is often deeply personal and vulnerable—just move on. There is no value in publicly tearing down someone's small, self-published work. Finally, always give credit. If a zine inspired you, mention it. If you collaborate with someone, shout them out. This community thrives on a web of interconnectedness and mutual appreciation.

Being a good community member is simple: be the kind of person you'd want to trade with, table next to, and get a package from. Be enthusiastic, be reliable, and be kind. That's it. That's the whole secret.

That stack of zines sitting in your room is more than just paper and ink. It's a key. It's a passport. It's an invitation. Each copy is a chance to connect with someone, to start a conversation, to find a kindred spirit. The act of creation was for you. The act of sharing is for everyone else. Now go unlock some doors.

You're a Zinester Now: Keep Creating, Keep Sharing

There you are, sitting on your floor, surrounded by a small, perfect stack of your creations. The smell of toner and paper is still hanging in the air. The whir of the photocopier has faded, the last staple has been punched. That stack of zines on your desk or your rug is no longer a dream or a pile of master pages; it's a real, tangible thing. It's a pile of potential conversations, of shared secrets, of tiny paper boats you're about to send out into the world.

This is the moment. The quiet, strange, electric moment after the making is done. It's easy to think of this as the end. You followed the steps, you wrestled the blank page into submission, you navigated the strange logic of imposition, and you emerged on the other side with a finished object. You did it. But this isn't the finish line. This is the starting line of a whole new race.

Because you're not just a person who made a zine. You're a zinester now. It's a subtle shift, but a powerful one. It's a new lens through which to see the world. It's an identity, a community, and a way of being. And the most important thing to know about being a zinester is that the work is never truly done. Thank goodness for that.

The End is Just the Beginning of Your Zine Journey

We tend to think of creative projects as having a clear beginning, middle, and end. You have an idea, you execute it, you release it, you move on. But zines defy that linear logic. Your first zine isn't a final exam that you've passed. It's a diary entry, a snapshot, a single frame in the long, messy, beautiful movie of your life and your interests. The person who made that zine is already changing, and the person who reads it will change you in return.

I still have copies of the first real zine I ever made. It's a chaotic, angsty, and deeply earnest perzine about feeling trapped in my hometown. The lettering is shaky, the collages are clumsy, and some of the poetry makes me physically cringe. For years, I was embarrassed by it. I saw only its flaws, its naivete. I saw it as a crude early attempt before I "got good." But I was missing the point entirely.

That zine wasn't a failed attempt at a masterpiece. It was a perfect artifact of who I was at that exact moment. It was a declaration that my story mattered, even if it was a story of teenage boredom and confusion. Holding it now is like looking at an old photograph. I don't see the technical flaws anymore. I see a kid who was figuring things out, who was finding a way to speak when they felt voiceless. It's a conversation with my former self. It reminds me where I came from.

Your zine is the same. Whether it's a fanzine about a niche horror movie, a collection of vegan recipes, or a raw, vulnerable perzine, it's a time capsule. The goal isn't to create a flawless, timeless object. The goal is to keep creating them. To build a library of your own evolution. Ten years from now, you will look back at this first zine and you won't see the crooked staple or the typo on page three. You'll see a brave person who had something to say and found a way to say it. And you'll be so, so proud of them.

Overcoming the Creative Slump: How to Keep the Ideas Flowing After Your First Zine

The exhilaration of finishing your first zine is often followed by a quiet, slightly panicked feeling. It's the creative equivalent of "What now?" You've poured so much energy and so many ideas into this one project that the well can feel completely dry. The pressure to make a second zine that's even better, smarter, or more polished than the first can be paralyzing. This is the infamous "second album syndrome," and it's a killer of momentum.

The secret to beating it is to remember the core ethos of zine making: the stakes are incredibly low. This isn't a record deal.

This isn't a book contract. The only barrier to entry is the cost of a few photocopies. You have nothing to lose. When I feel that pressure mounting, when the blank page feels like a spotlight instead of a playground, I have a few tricks I return to. The first is to go small.

Forget the 24-page, saddle-stitched epic you're imagining. Go back to the very beginning. Grab a single sheet of paper and make an 8-page mini-zine, just like we did in Chapter 5. Give yourself a one-hour time limit. The topic can be something ridiculously simple: everything you ate today, a list of songs stuck in your head, a review of the movie you watched last night, a rant about how your bus was late. The point isn't to create a great work of art. The point is to remind your brain and your hands what it feels like to make something. It's a creative reset button. More often than not, the simple act of finishing a tiny, silly project unsticks something bigger.

Another powerful antidote to the slump is collaboration. Zine making can feel like a solitary pursuit, but it doesn't have to be.

Find a friend—another zinester or even just a creative person you admire—and propose a split zine. Each of you creates half the content, and you combine it into a single issue. This immediately cuts your workload in half and, more importantly, introduces a new voice into your creative process. You'll be amazed at how someone else's ideas can spark your own, pushing you in directions you never would have gone alone. It turns a daunting task into a shared adventure.

And when all else fails, go back to the treasure hunt. Stop trying to generate ideas from thin air and go out into the world to collect them. Spend an afternoon in a library you've never visited. Go to a thrift store and buy the weirdest, most beaten-up paperback you can find for a dollar. Read the junk mail. Eavesdrop on conversations at a coffee shop. Your next zine is already out there, waiting in fragments. Your job isn't always to be a brilliant creator; sometimes it's just to be a curious collector. The inspiration worker likes it when you meet her halfway, and sometimes that means leaving your desk and letting the world write the zine for you.

A Call to Action: Start a Zine Club, Host a Reading, Teach a Friend

You now possess a form of magic. You know how to turn a blank page and a feeling into a tangible object that can travel across town or across the world. You know how to fold a single sheet of paper into a book. You know the secret language of imposition and the quiet art of the long-reach stapler. This knowledge is a gift, and the absolute best thing you can do with it is to give it away.

The true, lasting power of zines is not in the individual object, but in the community that forms around them. Zines are a conversation, and now it's your turn to invite more people to the party. This sounds like a grand, intimidating task, but it starts incredibly small. It starts with teaching one person. The next time a friend says, "Wow, you made this? How?"—show them.

Sit down with them with a piece of paper and show them the magic of the mini-zine fold. You will see a spark in their eyes. It is one of the most rewarding feelings in the world.

From there, the possibilities expand. What if you and that friend, and maybe one other, decided to meet once a month to work on your zines together? That's a zine club. It doesn't need a formal name or a public meeting place. It can be three people in a living room with glue sticks and snacks, sharing tips and holding each other accountable. This small circle of mutual support is the foundational atom of the entire zine ecosystem.

Maybe you get a little bolder. You could organize a zine reading. Again, this doesn't have to be a massive, publicly promoted event at a bookstore. It can be in your backyard. It can be five friends reading one page each from their latest zine. I remember my first zine reading; my hands were shaking so badly I could barely hold the pages, and my voice cracked. But when I looked up, the small crowd was nodding along. They got it. In that moment, the intensely personal, solitary act of writing became a shared, communal experience. It's terrifying, and it is absolutely essential.

By sharing your skills and creating these small pockets of community, you are doing the most important work a zinester can do. You are ensuring that this beautiful, weird, vital tradition continues. You are keeping the channels of self-expression open. You are actively building the world you want to live in—one where everyone has a voice, and everyone knows how to make copies.

A Final Thank You to the Zine Community, Past and Present

As you sit here, with this book in your hands and a head full of ideas, it's important to remember that you are not alone. You are part of a long, unbroken chain of rebels, dreamers, fanatics, and poets. You are the spiritual descendant of the science fiction fans of the 1930s, who were so passionate they couldn't wait for the mainstream press to publish their conversations. You are standing on the shoulders of the Beat poets, who mimeographed their verses because no publisher would touch them.

You carry the torch of the punks in the '70s and '80s, who used crooked staples and angry collages to build a global scene from scratch, proving that all you need is something to say and a way to make copies. You are continuing the fierce, world-changing work of the Riot Grrrls in the '90s, who used their perzines as manifestos, building networks of solidarity and challenging a culture that tried to silence them. They all said, in their own way, "If you won't publish us, we'll do it ourselves."

This book, and your journey as a zinester, would be impossible without them. And it would be impossible without the people who are doing the work right now. So, thank you to the distros—the people who run tables at fests, manage online shops, and pack mailers in their living rooms, all for the love of getting these little paper booklets into new hands. Thank you to the zine librarians, who painstakingly catalog, preserve, and champion this ephemeral art form, arguing for its place in our cultural history. Thank you to the zine fest organizers, who perform the logistical miracles required to bring hundreds of us together in a single, joyous, chaotic room.

And finally, thank you. Thank you for picking up this book. Thank you for being curious. Thank you for taking that leap, for picking up the scissors and the glue. By deciding to add your voice to the chorus, you become part of this history. You become one of the people who keeps the fire burning. Welcome. We are so, so glad you're here.

Appendix: Further Resources (Great Distros, Zine Libraries, and Online Archives)

The zine world can feel like a secret society, but the doors are wide open if you know where to look. This is by no means an exhaustive list, but rather a starting point—a treasure map to some of the key hubs of activity in the zine universe. Use these resources to find new zines to read, places to submit your own work, and inspiration for what's possible.

Zine Distros

Microcosm Publishing: Based in Portland, Oregon, Microcosm is one of the largest and longest-running distributors of zines and independent books. Their catalog is massive, and their focus on empowerment, skill-building, and social justice makes them a cornerstone of the community.

Brown Recluse Zine Distro: An excellent source for zines by people of color, with a mission to support and amplify marginalized voices within the DIY scene.

Sweet Candy Distro: Focuses on zines about feminism, gender, sexuality, and mental health. They have a fantastic selection of perzines and are a great example of a passion-driven distro.

Zine Libraries & Archives

The Internet Archive's Zine Collection: An incredible digital rabbit hole. They have scanned thousands of zines from across decades, covering every topic imaginable. It's an invaluable resource for research and inspiration, allowing you to flip through the pages of punk zines from the 80s or sci-fi fanzines from the 60s.

Barnard Zine Library: Located at Barnard College in New York City, this is one of the most prominent academic zine libraries, with a special focus on zines by women and non-binary creators. Many of their holdings are digitized and viewable online.

QZAP (The Queer Zine Archive Project): An online archive dedicated to preserving queer zines, past and present. Their mission is to make these materials accessible to a new generation of activists, artists, and historians.

Finding Zine Fests

Stolen Sharpie Revolution: This website, an extension of the iconic zine resource book of the same name, maintains one of the most comprehensive and up-to-date lists of zine fests happening around the world. It's the best place to start if you're looking for an event in your area.

So now it's over to you. The book ends here, but your story as a zinester is just getting started. Go make things. Go share them. Go find your people. And never, ever let anyone tell you that your story doesn't matter.

Somewhere out there, in a dusty corner of a record store or a cluttered table at a zine fest, a seventeen-year-old kid who is adrift in a sea of boredom is about to find your zine. The one with the hand-drawn cover and the crooked staples. They're going to pick it up, and it's going to feel like a secret just for them. It's going to be a tiny island of weirdness that makes them feel less alone. And they will have no idea that

Índice